Keys to the Mind

Learn How to
Hypnotize Anyone

and

Practice Hypnosis and
Hypnotherapy Correctly

Richard K. Nongard, LMFT/CCH
Nathan Thomas, CCH/MNLP

For orders other than by individual consumers, a discount is available on the purchase of 5 or more copies of individual titles for special markets or premium use.

For further details, please contact the publisher:

PeachTree Professional Education, Inc.
7107 S. Yale, Suite 370
Tulsa, OK 74136

(800) 390-9536
www.SubliminalScience.com

Keys to the Mind, Learn How to Hypnotize Anyone and Practice Hypnosis and Hypnotherapy Correctly

By Richard K. Nongard, LMFT/CCH
and Nathan Thomas, C.Ht.

Edited by Paula Duncan

Cover Design by Ricky Nongard

ISBN 978-0-557-09784-5

PRAISE

Welcome to the wonderful world of hypnosis . . . with Richard Nongard as your guide, you can't miss. Richard knows his way around hypnosis better than most hypnotists who've been doing it twice as many years as himself, and he's been doing hypnosis for a lot of years . . . so, he obviously knows a lot and he's kind enough to invite you along and share his knowledge with you. Nathan Thomas may not be quite as long in the tooth as Richard, but he's a gifted young man who is going places in the world of hypnosis. Knowing you've got two skilled hypnotic guides on your journey, you can rest assured that with the material covered in this book, you'll not only unlock the keys to the mind, but open doors into a fascinating and wonderful future as a hypnotist . . . and . . . more!

~ Brian David Phillips, PhD
President, Society of Experiential Trance
www.BrianDavidPhillips.com

After reviewing this book, I'm glad to say Richard Nongard and Nathan Thomas have put together a brilliant educational work on the hypnosis profession. This book is an invalueable asset and resource, containing a wealth of carefully crafted information for both the novice "newbie" as well as enlightened insights to inspire and guide seasoned professionals.

This work insightfully covers a wide variety of hypnosis techniques, topics and methods, while skillfully ensuring the of avoidance of pitfalls. This tome is a must-have for the library of any serious hypnotist or hypno-enthusiast.

~ John Cerbone
aka *"The Trance-Master"*
www.Trance-Master.com

A word about copyright infringement and e-books....

If you are the original purchaser of this book, we want to thank-you for you purchase. By buying this product and others you have recognized the unique value that creators of quality products deserve. On the other hand, if this file was downloaded by a torrent, distributed from a website not associated with the authors or publishers, or has been emailed to you by someone else, you have denied the creators of this unique and valuable product the compensation they deserve.

If this is the case, please visit **www.SubliminalScience.com** to obtain a legal copy of this text.

Do not participate in illegal file sharing or distribution of this text.

ALSO AVAILABLE

www.SubliminalScience.com

Textbooks

- Inductions and Deepeners, Styles and Approaches for Effective Hypnosis
- Understanding Hypnosis and Self-Hypnosis, an easy to follow book about hypnotism

DVD Instruction

- How to Write Effective Hypnosis Scripts and Suggestions
- Speed Trance: Instant Hypnotic Inductions
- Mastering Hypnotic Power: Using Hypnotic Phenomena
- Learn Hypnosis: How to Hypnotize Anyone
- Learn how to use Progressive Muscle Relaxation (PMR) for more effective therapy and as a tool for hypnotic induction
- How to do Autogenic Training: Techniques for taking control of the mind-body connection
- NLP Essentials: Strategies for Personal Power and Influence
- Hypnotic Inductions: Methods that Work (Vol 1)
- Inductions and Deepeners (Vol 2)
- Learn How to Do Self Hypnosis
- Meditation Techniques for the Beginner

Audio CDs

- Therapeutic Relaxation - Distress Tolerance Training
- Insomnia, Quit Smoking, Weight Loss, Pain Management, Overcoming Lost Love, Test-Taking Anxiety, Better Golf, Building Confidence, and many other topics

Professional Resources

- Richard Nongard's Crash Course on Building a Profitable Practice - A Guidebook and DVD Video for Professional Success
- The NSRI: Nongard Strengths and Resources Inventory

ABOUT THE AUTHORS

Richard K. Nongard is a Licensed Marriage and Family Therapist, a Certified Clinical Hypnotherapist and a Certified Personal Fitness Trainer, and holds degrees in both Ministry and Counseling.

A popular keynote presenter and conference speaker, Richard provides accredited continuation education and advanced skills training to hypnotists, psychotherapists, education professionals and criminal justice organizations around the globe on subjects related to clinical hypnosis practice, suicide, anxiety, depression, personality disorders, drug, alcohol and tobacco addiction, domestic violence, fitness and family health.

He is the developer of the QuitSuccess® Tobacco Cessation Treatment Program used by agencies and hospitals across the US, as well as several professional assessment tools and therapeutic client workbooks, and he is the acclaimed author of five clinical practice textbooks.

Solving problems by focusing on existing client strengths is the hallmark of Richard's approach.

Nathan Thomas, C.Ht., is the co-founder of the International Association of Teenage Hypnotists. Ambitious and dedicated, Nathan is a master practitioner of neuro-linguistic techniques and language patterns, and is a world-renown contributor to the field of hypnosis.

Nathan's blog, found at **www.KeysToTheMind.com**, is an amazing resource for any level of hypnosis professional. From training material reviews to new methods and approaches, you will find new learnings to practice and enjoy.

INTRODUCTION

THE JOURNEY BEGINS

Hello and welcome to *Keys to the Mind, Learn How to Hypnotize Anyone and Practice Hypnosis and Hypnotherapy Correctly.* You are now beginning the journey towards becoming a hypnotist and acquiring an effective array of clinical hypnosis skills, but before we dive right into the 'how to,' let us begin with a little introduction. This book is authored by myself, Richard Nongard, alongside Nathan Thomas. I am a Licensed Marriage and Family Therapist, a Certified Clinical Hypnotherapist, and a Certified Personal Fitness Trainer, with over 20 years experience working professionally in the field of hypnosis and offering hypnosis training courses worldwide.

Nathan Thomas is a Certified Hypnotist and NLP practitioner regarded throughout the world as an expert in the field of hypnosis. He launched and runs the International Association for Teenage Hypnotists and has trained hundreds of people in the art and science of hypnosis, both online and face-to- face. Nathan is the co-author of this text and has been a huge help in researching and composing the material you will soon be enjoying.

We would like to thank you for purchasing this book and are excited to be able to share our knowledge with you. By the time you have reviewed all of the material in this text, you will be well on your way to becoming a hypnotist - you will have the basic skills necessary to hypnotize a person, be able to lead them through a healing process, and understand how to awaken them properly when the session is complete.

Clinical Hypnosis is a valid intervention endorsed by both national and international medical and psychological associations for well over 50 years. If you have a clinical background in the helping professions – social work, counseling, nursing, medical doctor - you should find yourself ahead of the learning curve and happy to know that the skills of hypnosis can be easily integrated into your existing therapeutic approaches for helping clients to maximize their potential, especially in the area of brief therapy.

For those of you with no experience from a clinical perspective in the counseling or medical professions, my guess is that you are probably a person who enjoys helping other people. This is great, because hypnosis helps promote healing. Training in clinical hypnosis provides one of those rare opportunities where we can learn a skill that can actually help change a person's life for the better. I am not a person who believes that only those who have a degree in clinical psychology should be able to provide hypnosis and services. I believe that all people with an interest in helping others should be given the skills to do so effectively.

When writing a single educational text about hypnosis, in order to make sure all the bases are covered and that the instruction is reasonably complete, the authors must assume that their average readers have little or no prior experience with hypnosis. Nathan and I have worked hard to fulfill this obligation by including as much fundamental content as possible within these pages. However, we are well aware that many of our readers are already experienced hypnotists seeking to enhance their existing skills, and we feel confident that those of you with more training will also find this book to be quite valuable and useful to your overall knowledge base.

Happy reading and learning!

Richard K. Nongard, LMFT/CCH
Nathan Thomas, C.Ht.

CHAPTER 1

What is Hypnosis?

Hypnosis can be utilized in many ways for many purposes. This book centers around using hypnosis as a form of therapy, known as hypnotherapy or clinical hypnosis, for the purpose of helping people to heal and find solutions to the problems that they experience.

So that you can develop a solid understanding of what hypnosis really is and how it works, and to firmly lead you away from misconceptions often created by the media, let us begin by addressing a few concepts before we get into the core material. *Bare with us, we promise that you will be learning how to actually hypnotize someone sooner than you think.*

Hypnosis is a manifestation of natural phenomena that all of us experience in day-to-day life. There is nothing mystical about hypnosis. There is no Svengali-like magical power that the hypnotist must possess in order to help an individual. In fact, it probably would not be possible to have that type of power and truly be beneficial and helpful, because such dynamics would create an unequal relationship.

We all experience hypnotic phenomena in the course of a normal day: when we seem to 'zone out' while performing a habitual task like brushing our teeth, or seem to be on 'autopilot' when driving to work every day. Hypnosis is a safe and natural process, and can be an extremely powerful, fast-acting intervention. It can help people break free of their old problems so quickly that it leaves other healing arts in the dust.

Throughout this book you will often read the word 'trance.' We will address this in more detail later, but for now just think of trance as a state of hyper-suggestibility, where the critical or conscious part of the mind is less active, allowing the subconscious part of the mind to absorb and accept suggestions and ideas. When you realize that the unconscious mind makes up about approximately 90% of our overall brain power, it's easier to see how trance can certainly be such a powerful state.

My experience with hypnosis goes back quite a few years. As an undergraduate student, I took a job working in a chiropractor's office, and as part of my duties I was instructed to perform progressive muscle relaxation (PMR) inductions on clients. Now, back then I didn't recognize PMR as an 'induction' or ascribe a 'hypnosis' label to the process, but every day at the office I was unwittingly hypnotizing people and giving them the skills to relax and physically heal. Once I realized exactly what I was doing and how and why it worked so well, I studied hypnosis extensively. I then learned to integrate it into numerous areas of my professional work, and I utilize it daily in my personal life.

In addition to being a licensed marriage and family therapist and having a strong background as a substance abuse counselor, I am also certified as a personal fitness trainer. Hypnosis can easily be incorporated into sports psychology and is used effectively for helping a person to achieve peak levels of performance in any field.

Over the years I have worked with criminal justice clients, addicted clients, families, adolescents, children and adults, and frequently I find myself drawing upon my experiences in hypnosis to provide interventions for helping clients to manage the physical mani-festations of their emotions, to enhance health and wellness, to change self-destructive subconscious patterns and to learn new patterns for promoting healthy lifestyle and behavioral choices.

Clinical Hypnosis offers a particularly useful set of skills that can be applied to help solve or alter a variety of situations and problems that we experience every day.

In addition to my professional experience, hypnosis has had a huge positive influence on my personal life. I succeeded at smoking cessation a number of years ago (the number one reason clients seek out a clinical hypnotist), and also conquered my fear of flying.

Like most people who are afraid to fly, I would rationalize my fear: Why would I get into a metal tube, hurtling through the atmosphere at 600 miles an hour, when I could simply hop into a car and drive, and have the opportunity to see America along the way?

I overcame my fear of flying in large part by implementing the methods of therapeutic hypnosis, and today I fly all over the world. These days, when I find myself on an extremely long and boring flight, I utilize trance and hypnotic techniques in order to help me get through it. This process produces three benefits: one, it makes the time pass much faster; two, it makes the experience more productive; and three, I am far more comfortable and this, in turn, makes the passengers around me more comfortable. Many of you have probably suffered through flights next to someone who was noticeably high-strung, nervous or lacked relaxation techniques, and you know it's not a pleasant experience.

It is important to realize that if you want to practice clinical hypnosis to help others achieve their goals, you should experience hypnosis for yourself. It's far easier to assist others - effectively - when you are intimately familiar with the process by practicing the same skills in your own day-to-day life.

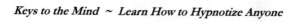

Hypnosis and Hypnotherapy

Before we go any further, let's take a few minutes and look at these two words: Hypnosis and Hypnotherapy. People often ask me, "Hey, Richard, is there a difference between hypnosis and hypno-therapy?" and you may be wondering the same thing.

In this particular training text, when I use the words hypnosis or hypnotherapy, the two can be used interchangeably. However, do I believe there is actually a difference between the two terms? Yes, I certainly I do.

Hypnosis itself is not a therapeutic process. Hypnotherapy, I believe, is a therapeutic process built upon a foundation of helping, of empathy, and of sincerely desiring to help people make changes, feel positive, and accomplish their goals in life. Hypnosis is a state of natural phenomena, and a vehicle or tool for providing hypno-therapy. Hypnotherapy is the process of bringing about that hypnotic trance state, and the hypnotist is simply the person who is helping another person to experience an induced highlight of the natural trance-phenomena we all experience every day.

Anyone can perform hypnosis.

I have many friends who are stage hypnotists, and I have actually done some stage performances myself. Stage hypnosis performance does not require a background in clinical psychology; people from all different career backgrounds can become a stage hypnotist.

Stage hypnosis does require learning how to manage a crowd, the basic strategies of induction and putting together a couple of simple, silly scripts, but that's about it. Whether or not they are a good stage performer and use their skills responsibly, ethically and effectively is an entirely different matter, but truly, performing hypnosis is not something that requires empathy, respect or even care of another individual. Now, I hope that they do have all of those things, because if not, I believe they would be using hypnosis irresponsibly, and it is these human qualities and personal elements that make for a good hypnotist and stage hypnosis show.

I once met a stage hypnotist at a comedy club; I went up to him after the show, introduced myself and talked to him a little bit. He was probably about 50 or 55 years old, and I asked him how he learned to do hypnosis. He said, "When I was 8 years old, I sent for a booklet I saw advertised in the back of a comic book on how to hypnotize somebody. I got it, tried it, and hypnotized my sister." He had paid 50 cents for the secret of hypnosis, and has been doing it every day since he was in grade school.

My point is certainly not to knock stage hypnotists, but simply to emphasize that anyone can hypnotize another person.

I am often asked if a person, who is in trance state, can interact - can they talk? And the answer is yes, they most certainly can. If you have ever seen hypnotized subjects interacting and completing assigned tasks at a stage show, there should be no question that they can engage in conversation in the office.

During the course of hypnotherapy we want to find out information about our clients in order to be a more effective helper. We will listen to their needs and ask questions during the hypnotherapy session. Clinical hypnosis practice involves interviewing and assessing clients, teaching specific skills, meeting them at their particular point of need, allowing them to verbalize what those needs are and establishing where they are making progress. By doing such it should become clear that clinical hypnosis is not necessarily a one-sided endeavor; it is a highly interactive process.

Just as a stage hypnotist will hypnotize a group of people at one time up on stage, it is also possible to do a clinical hypnosis session with more than one person at a time. I often have husbands and wives together in my counseling office for a two-part hypnotherapy program. During the first session I probably spend about 30 minutes interviewing them for assessment purposes, then spend an additional 20 or 30 minutes going through what would be considered a traditional hypnotherapy session. The second visit generally consists of almost 40 minutes in traditional talk-therapy, cognitive-behavioral therapy, and assessment, because I teach them specific strategies, and ultimately we spend only about 20 or 25 minutes engaged in hypnosis.

What you can learn from the above example is that hypnotherapy is a modality of treatment that can incorporate elements not usually categorized as hypnosis. Hypnosis, in and of itself, is not inherently therapeutic; it can be used for entertainment, incorporated into sales, used to enhance persuasion or self-development, and is often experienced accidentally, as mentioned earlier, while driving or going about mundane tasks. Hypnotherapy, on the other hand, is the structured use of hypnosis in a professional environment, with the intention of creating specific remedial or generative changes.

Why use hypnosis? Why use hypnotherapy?

Aren't there other methods of helping people solve problems – addiction, anxiety, depression, sexual dysfunction, confidence and self-esteem, focus and concentration, headaches, insomnia, weight gain, etc - that are effective? Certainly there are, and I'm not going to knock any other methods.

For example, I think 12-Step programs – Alcoholics Anonymous, Narcotics Anonymous, Cocaine Addicts Anonymous and others – are significantly profound and effective for aiding the recovery of addiction. The *Big Book* of Alcoholics Anonymous was put together by the first 100 members of the program. As alcoholics themselves, they understood the issues that others like them faced, and they developed twelve steps designed to help themselves and others lead the path to physical, emotional and spiritual healing, and this process works for those who work it.

Hypnosis, however, is another fantastic tool for addressing addiction-related problems. Withdrawal is a physical process, and hypnosis is a skill that helps a person to manage their physical experiences through the power of the mind. With or without incorporating the 12-Step modality into treatment, we still know that hypnosis is a powerful and effective way to both change subconscious behavioral associations and teach new skills for managing the physical symptoms of withdrawal.

But every individual has different needs, so as a counselor, when someone comes to me with an alcohol or drug addiction problem, I assess which are the best interventions I can provide to help the individual experience relief from their problems, be it via hypnosis, the 12 Steps, cognitive-behavioral methods, or any other strategy designed to help resolve their specific issues.

The important concept here is that as healers, we find out what works, what is effective, and we use it. Or, if we are not qualified or experienced with the likely best method, we refer to those who are.

Let us consider a contrary example from a typical psychiatrist's office: A client comes in and claims to be suffering from depression. The psychiatrist, being a medical doctor and therefore oriented towards medications, as a first line of intervention, would tell the depressed person that they should take an antidepressant pill. But research shows us that if a person engages in cardiovascular exercise for 40 minutes a day, 3 or 4 times a week, for six weeks or longer, they are exponentially more likely to experience a decrease in the symptoms associated with major depression than if they take antidepressant medications.

It used to be believed that hypnosis was contra-indicated for depression, but in reality this is not true at all. Michael Yapko has written a great book called *Hypnosis and Treating Depression*, a well-researched text showing the efficacy of hypnosis as an intervention for major depression. Happiness is, after all, in the mind.

I am not opposed to antidepressant medications, and I have met a lot of people who, particularly during times of catastrophic depression, have been stabilized on medications. However, when someone comes to me and says, "Hey, I'm depressed and I need a resolution for my depression," one of the first interventions I will prescribe is that they engage in exercise on a regular basis for a period of six weeks or longer, because I know that they will feel better as a result. Then I will most likely include hypnosis in my repertoire of intervention strategies.

Is hypnosis safe?

Hypnosis is safe; there are no negative side effects from hypnosis. Well, I suppose there are some inherent risks, just like there are with driving an automobile or flying on an airplane or living life in general, which could happen during a state of hypnosis and could be potentially harmful to a person. For example, it is possible that someone could, in a state of trance, fall out of their chair. And perhaps there is a chance for some physical discomfort during a state of muscular catalepsy; however that is much more likely to occur during a stage hypnosis show than in the therapy office.

The worry I hear most often concerns a therapist abusing a client, however I do not think a hypnotherapist is any more likely to abuse their client than any other form of therapist. Contrary to some misbeliefs, hypnotherapy clients do not yield control to the hypnotist; the client maintains control of their own mind and thoughts and they make their own decisions.

Of course there is always the risk for abreaction: intense emotional experiences which a person does not expect, does not enjoy, and did not want to experience during the process of hypnosis. However, these situations are quite rare and are easily dealt with by the competent hypnotist. (We will discuss abreaction in great detail later on.)

Does hypnosis work?

Not only is hypnosis safe, it works. Research shows that hypnosis is an effective treatment for weight loss, smoking cessation and depression. It has been shown to increase success in recovery from burns, cancer, irritable bowel syndrome and numerous other ailments. It is also highly effective for generative improvement, increasing thought processes and productivity. In short, yes, hypnosis works.

John Stossel, one of TV's greatest skeptics, released a book called, *Myths, Lies and Downright Stupidity,* in which he set out to debunk many myths, lies, and legends in our society, and one of the subjects he covered was hypnosis. On page 215 he wrote, "Just when my skeptic's antennae convince me I always know bunk when I see it, I get fooled. I assumed hypnosis in medicine was one more con game... 'Hypnotherapy will help you lose weight!' C'mon, if it worked, there wouldn't be all those overweight people around. Truth: Hypnosis works -- if you let it!"

Does hypnosis solve everyone's problems all of the time? No. There has never been and there never will be a one-size-fits-all approach that will fix every issue, every time. Just like there are different modalities of intervention for different medical, psychological, and spiritual difficulties, hypnosis is a tool which will be effective with most of our clients much of the time, but not necessarily all.

What are the Benefits of Hypnosis?

Hypnosis is Natural

Whenever possible, why wouldn't we seize the opportunity to provide a natural treatment to help a person - without toxicity, without drugs, without liver damage, without the side effects of chemotherapy or other medications? Of course hypnosis does not always keep a person from needing other medical interventions, however, sometimes clients are so successful with hypnosis that they are able to give up higher risks and more toxic, harmful protocols that were only useful to them in the short term, not the long run.

I am certainly not advocating that everyone quit using all medications and other methods of treatment and focus exclusively on hypnosis; I am simply saying that hypnosis is a safe, effective and natural treatment that can often help enhance other approaches to treating their medical needs. So why not give it a shot?

Another benefit of hypnosis is that it feels good. The state of hypnotic trance is a highly pleasant state to experience, often accompanied by feelings of deep peace, relaxation and physical and mental comfort. As healers, our job is essentially to make people happy, and what better way to do than with a method that feels good?

The process of hypnosis is also highly effective for teaching skills that our clients can take with them when they leave our office, to carry them through the next problem that they experience.

Consider the client who experiences panic attacks. Panic is a very physical emotion. In fact, if you look up panic attacks in the DSM-IV (the Diagnostic *and Statistical Manual of Mental Disorders, fourth edition,* by the American Psychological Association), you will see that the first eight symptoms listed are all physical in nature: butterflies in the stomach, trembling, shakiness, sweating, feelings of choking, chills, feeling dizzy, and so on. Hypnosis teaches the skills that can help overcome these symptoms: to take a deep breath and to let it out slowly, to feel the oxygen fill their lungs, to feel their heart rate slow down, and the physical difference between tension and relaxation. In teaching our clients these skills, we teach them how to solve not only the initial problem they came to us for help with (panic attacks), but also how to handle a host of other obstacles they may experience later in life.

Hypnosis Works Quickly

In the era of managed care with limited time and limited resources, both clients and therapists are looking for brief therapy modalities. In the 'olden days,' Sigmund Freud's basic idea of treatment was complete personality restructuring; he envisioned a therapy process that extended two or three times a week over a period of ten to fifteen years. These days we often don't have ten or fifteen sessions, much less years, to bring a client up from hysterical misery to even common depression. Today, our goal instead is to provide interventions to help our clients to quit smoking, lose weight, experience healing, manage stress to achieve success, and generally find relief from the painful and difficult situations they have in life, and to do so quickly.

Hypnotherapy reprograms the subconscious and teaches new skills that a person can actually apply in multiple day-to-day life experiences, which of course makes hypnotherapy a brief intervention strategy. Most hypnotherapists will tell you that typically one, two, or three sessions is all they need to realize success with most clients for most issues. *Gut Magazine*, the journal of gastroenterology, came out with clinical research in 1997 affirming the efficacy of using hypnosis to treat irritable bowel syndrome (IBS), a long-suffering, miserable condition. They recommend a seven-session protocol of hypnosis; brief therapy.

Now that you have a reasonably good idea of the benefits of hypnosis, and are beginning to understand what hypnosis actually is, let us leap right into this book's guiding question: How do you hypnotize someone?

CHAPTER 2

The
Who, What, Where, When and Why of Hypnosis

All hypnosis is essentially self-hypnosis. As a hypnotist, I am facilitating the natural process of helping a person to experience trance. It is not something that I do *to* someone; instead, it is something that I am doing *with* them. In fact, even when I am recording hypnosis CD's or performing hypnosis live on stage, I find myself in my own zone of trance. This is because hypnosis is a natural process, and the hypnotist, just like the client, will find themselves in varying levels of trance during the hypnotic procedure.

As I mentioned earlier, hypnosis is a natural occurrence that we all experience at one time or another throughout the day. Think about the first five minutes before you fall asleep at night: you know you could open your eyes if you wanted to, but it feels so good that you simply want to keep them shut. That in-between-awake-and-asleep time is a natural trance state.

Hypnosis often carries with it a function of time distortion, a fairly common hypnotic phenomenon. You get into your car after work and you drive towards home, and by the time you arrive there ten or fifteen minutes later, you think, "Wow! I don't remember my drive from the office to my house; I just sort of showed up." Your subconscious mind was guiding your drive home, whilst your conscious mind was allowed to relax and 'zone (trance) out' for a while and focus on more interesting subjects. Hypnosis is the opposite of meditation where the person is trying to clear their mind. Instead, hypnosis is an induced state of total concentration and focus.

Hypnotizing someone simply involves leading them through the natural phenomena that they have already experienced in day-to-day life.

When performing hypnosis, we harness this natural phenomenon through what is called the hypnotic process. The hypnotic process involves 5 stages: a time of pre-talk (explanation), the induction (going into trance), followed by deepeners (increasing the trance state), then the suggestion phase (therapeutic ideas), and finally the awakening or dehypnotizing.

As we take our clients through this 5-stage hypnotic process, we will use techniques such as visualization, interaction, kinesthetic experiences, and specific word choices designed to address the subconscious mind in much the same way that they experience trance in their everyday life. When you are done with this book, you will be able to go through these five stages and perform a variety of different induction and deepening techniques.

Defining Hypnosis

According to the U.S. Dept. of Education, Human Services Division,
  hypnosis is:

> "The by-pass of the critical factor of the conscious
> mind (a person's analytical and judgmental ability)
> followed by the establishment of acceptable selective
> thinking."

So that this short but useful statement by the US Government
makes a little more sense, a brief explanation is likely in order. The
mind has four different divisions: the Conscious Mind, the Critical
Factor, the Subconscious Mind, and the Unconscious Mind.

The Unconscious Mind is where our instincts are - the things
we intrinsically know from birth and throughout life - and it
protects us reflexively.

The Unconscious Mind controls the autonomic nervous
system, respiration and heartbeat. Its learning is capacity
limited, but Pavlov demonstrated that it can be impacted
when he made dogs salivate to a ringing bell. This is known
as classical conditioning.

The Subconscious Mind starts out empty, then, as we
grow and learn, the unlimited capacity database stores
our experiences and perceptions, which then create our
personality, emotions, learned responses, beliefs and habits.
These ideas and concepts become 'embedded' and are then
highly resistant to change.

The Subconscious Mind uses its database to protect against
known threats, and to motivate us to fulfill our needs. This
is the concept of Tabula Rasa - experiences and learning are
written upon us. Some have called this *temperament* (Jung).
The subconscious mind resists conscious change, but hypnosis
can have immediate effect on the subconscious (Banyan).

The Conscious Mind is analytical and logical, and is where we spend most of our time. The Conscious Mind protects us against immediate threats and is where we problem-solve - assess situations and implement resolutions; it evaluates the specific concern or issue that has its attention at the moment. It then makes choices and decisions for day-to-day functioning.

In the Conscious Mind, thoughts that are considered to be more important will replace those of less importance. Conscious change is temporal, because the capacity is limited. This makes subconscious reprogramming more effective.

The Conscious Mind is also where "will power" comes into play. But as you may have noticed, quite often our will power is not powerful enough, and we often quickly revert back to our old habits and ways. This is due to the influence of the Critical Factor section of our mind.

The Critical Factor is the gate-keeper between the Sub-conscious Mind and the Conscious Mind. It functions as a filter for new information coming in from the Conscious Mind, and compares/contrasts it to the existing database of beliefs in the Subconscious Mind. When the newly introduced data does not jibe with the existing database, the Critical Factor rejects it, by not allowing changes in emotional or behavioral responses to occur. This is why it is so difficult to break habits or change our beliefs.

"The bypass of the critical factor" of the Government's definition refers to the hypnotic processes' release of the imposed limiting beliefs - essentially disarming the Critical Factor - which then allows emotional or behavioral hypnotic suggestions to pass through the Conscious Mind and into the Subconscious Mind.

"The establishment of acceptable selective thinking" refers to the actual creation of new beliefs in the Subconscious Mind through suggestibility, a sort of reprogramming, which allows you to break habits, change perceptions, and create new auto-responses to situations.

Probably the best example of how these different brain components work together is in relation to smoking. If I've been smoking cigarettes for 20 or 30 years, my mind subconsciously believes certain things to be true that simply are not, such as that I'm going to freak out if I don't get nicotine. My mind believes that if I'm in a car, I must light a cigarette, or that if I just ate dinner, I need that after-dinner smoke. Over 20, 30 or 40 years of smoking, my subconscious mind has learned things that are not true and has incorporated these inaccurate beliefs or cognitive-errors into my everyday living.

Hypnosis, however, allows our subconscious mind to learn new or healthier patterns by bypassing the critical factor and allowing into the subconscious mind a new set of beliefs, behaviors and options.

The conscious mind is the thinking part of the mind, and it is interesting to note that the thinking part is actually the smallest part of the mind. Imagine an iceberg submerged under the ocean. Above water, the iceberg only shows about 10% of its full bulk; 90% is underneath the water line.

Likewise, the conscious mind consumes only about 10% of our mind power or capacity. Therefore, about 90% of what the mind does is subconscious. In the morning before you get up, you don't have to think about which leg you put in your pants first, you just get up and put your pants on. When you go to get a drink of water from a water fountain, you don't have to consciously decide, "I think I will move my arm muscles first and my thumb muscles next;" you just automatically do these things in the proper order with the help of the unconscious mind. We do these things automatically because over the years, through both nature and nurture – experience – we have learned physically, psychologically, socially, communicatively how to do these things.

The conscious mind is the part of the mind that our attention is drawn to at any particular time. They say that our conscious mind is only able to experience about seven different things at the same time; if an eighth piece of information is added, it will be rejected. Now, the subconscious may actually absorb it, even while the conscious mind is rejecting it.

For example: Let's say you are busy cooking dinner. You are stirring a big pot of beans on the stove. You are putting cornbread muffins in the oven. You don't want to make a mess or burn yourself. You want the butter soft during the meal so you're getting the butter out of the refrigerator. In the meantime, the phone rings, so you answer. It's your sister talking about her new job. You are still looking in the refrigerator for the butter, and your son comes into the kitchen. He stands right next to you and talks to you. He sees you nod thinks that you are listening to him and hearing what he says. He talks and talks while you are on the phone with your sister, finding the butter, stirring the beans on the stove, setting the timer for the muffins, getting bowls and spoons from the cabinets and drawers, and doing all the things related to dinner preparation. You have seven things going on at that moment. Your son talking at you is number eight. You find the butter. Now your mind is only doing six things because you found the butter. At that moment, you look over and you realize someone is talking to you. You focus on your son and say, "What?"

Even though they were talking to you, you didn't really even know they were there until you found the butter, until your conscious mind got rid of something so that eighth piece of information could occupy the seventh spot. This is the conscious mind in action, processing only those things few that we have immediate awareness of at any given time.

Our subconscious mind is the part that stores all of our life learning experiences and creates functional associations for daily living, both healthy and unhealthy. For the cigarette smoker, an association may be, "(Because) I get in my car and I (must) light up a cigarette." Sometimes they will light a cigarette when they already have another one burning in an ashtray, because they automatically light up cigarettes after certain associative cues, even if they don't necessarily smoke them. This is the part of the mind that we will reprogram using hypnosis, so that actions become consistent with healthy release, rather than consistent with unhealthy release.

(I know that at this point you're looking for the 'one, two, three - this is how you do it explanation,' but trust me, while you are reading and learning more about what hypnosis really is and how and why it works, you are learning the fundamentals you need for the one, two, three part.)

The Three Laws Of Hypnosis

In order for us to hypnotize someone, we must understand the laws of hypnosis. These 'laws' are guiding principles which you should endeavor to adhere to as much as possible when doing hypnosis.

The first law of hypnosis is that the person being hypnotized must have a clear image of what the process and results will feel like and be like.

In order to successfully achieve change, the client must be able to clearly visualize, imagine or at least understand what the final result of that change will be. In the counseling world, this is known as informed consent, explaining what to expect both during the therapeutic process and in the end.

For example, when I give someone my four-part smoking cessation CD series, I usually engage in a conversation like this one with a client named Sue:

Sue asks, "Will these help me to quit smoking?"

I say, "Yes, absolutely."

Sue asks, "How long after I listen to them until I quit smoking?"

My answer is, "As soon as you start listening to them, you have stopped smoking." (By the way, that is suggestive language.)

Sue asks, "Do I have to listen to them over and over again in order to remain a non-smoker?"

I reply, "No, you don't need to listen to them over and over again to remain a non-smoker. Most people find that if they do listen to them over and over again, it is beneficial because they learn specific useful strategies and skills. You will, in fact, be a non-smoker when you make the commitment to listen to all four of these CD's."

Since our client must have a clear image of the intended result, I then asked Sue to picture in her mind of listening to the CD's and being a non-smoker. When she took a minute to create that mental picture, there was no doubt about it - she went home and put on that first CD, and from that moment on she was a non-smoker.

Our clients need a clear picture of what the outcome will be, to visualize themselves experiencing success. The client in pain needs to visualize that he is not experiencing pain, the client who needs to lose weight needs to visualize themselves thinner and healthier, and the person who smokes cigarettes needs to visualize that they are living life not smoking cigarettes. This brief process will substantially increase your therapeutic success.

The second law states that when the subject's will and imagination (belief) are in conflict, the imagination will always win.

Another way of stating this is that when the conscious and the unconscious minds conflict, the unconscious will always win. This concept actually gives us a great advantage, because it means that a client's rational side can give way to imagination. When the rational side lets down its guard, the critical factor can be side-stepped, and old, unhealthy ways of living can be replaced with new, healthy ways.

The third law of hypnosis is that a suggestion is more likely to be accepted when it is tied to a positive emotion or affect, with which the subject can identify.

Simply put, suggestions that are positive are more likely to be accepted than those that are negative. For example, in smoking cessation, one could use negative suggestions in the form of aversion therapy: "The next time you smell a cigarette burning, you will become nauseatingly ill. The smell of smoke will sicken your stomach. It will irritate your nostrils and give you a headache."

It has been my experience that people generally do not accept negative suggestions, but they will accept positive suggestions. Instead of telling a client that they will feel nasty if they see a cigarette or smell cigarette smoke, I say that they 'enjoy breathing fresh air, they feel good when they can feel the oxygen flowing in through the nostrils and into the lungs; fresh, healing oxygen carrying nutrients throughout their body.'

As we create suggestive scripts to help our clients, we want to always accentuate the positive rather than the negatives, and for the most part, we want to avoid aversion therapy all together. Instead, we will replace old patterns of behavior with new patterns that are healthy and exciting. For example, here's a therapeutic suggestion lesson I learned from my history as a drug and alcohol counselor: When a client would ask, "Are you going to tell me that I can't ever use drugs and alcohol again?" I always answer with a firm 'No!' for two reasons. One, the answer confuses them and creates conflict in the mind, like a pattern interrupt, and therefore also creates the instant opportunity to impart new ideas into the subconscious, and two, instead of focusing on the negative of never using drugs again we want the client to focus on the positives of living life happy and healthy without the need for chemicals.

I want my clients who are recovering from addictions to enjoy what they did last night, to like who they were with last night. I want them to enjoy living life and not miss any of it by being drunk or stoned or high. I don't want my clients to give up drinking; I want them to start loving life clear-headed.

Positive suggestions are much more likely to be received by the subconscious than negative or aversion therapy oriented suggestions. People are also more likely to accept 'do' suggestions rather than 'do not' suggestions. Your suggestions – the words you use - create images and thoughts inside the subconscious of your clients. In order to 'not' think about doing something, you must first think about doing it, so always try to frame your suggestions in a positive, pro-active, 'in-the-now' manner wherever possible.

Make sure you fully understand these three simple laws of hypnosis, and use them in your practice; they will make your hypnosis practice exponentially more powerful and effective.

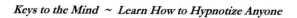

Ericksonian Hypnosis

I am asked quite often about the difference between Ericksonian hypnotherapy and other approaches. Many people have heard the term Ericksonian Hypnosis, but they don't fully understand what it means, or how it's relevant to practicing hypnotherapy. I am well trained in Ericksonian hypnotherapy, having studied under a master hypnotist in California and also in Germany with a septuagenarian psychologist who was trained in Arizona by Milton Erickson himself. I also spent some time in Toronto learning neuro-linguistic programming and NLP's approaches to hypnosis and hypnotherapy. And, having received education from these many different perspectives, I would encourage you to do the same.

Ericksonian Hypnosis comes from the study of Dr. Milton Erickson's work during the nineteen-fifties and -sixties. Erickson was a psychiatrist and probably studied and researched more on clinical hypnosis that anyone else before or since, and has been considered one of the greatest hypnotists of our time. He brought the field of hypnosis to professional attention and founded the one of the first clinical hypnosis professional associations in the 60's, and the Milton Erickson Foundation in Arizona is still actively providing hypnosis education to mental health professionals today.

Erickson believed that trance is a natural phenomenon, that we are always in one state of trance or another, and therefore that induction is not necessary. His view was that clients come to us ready to begin doing the work, and so all that is needed is to simply facilitate a deeper level of trance through conversation, without the need for a formal process.

Ericksonian hypnosis is particularly interactive. It is much more like traditional therapy, in that a person is in a state of trance and the hypnotist will interview and ask questions and really engage in the assessment process during the trance state.

Erickson taught that psychic healing occurs without the need for directive commands, that people have within themselves all the knowledge they already need in order to solve their problems, and during the course of a trance experience they are able to bring those preexisting internal realizations to the forefront of their mind and begin the healing and problem-solving process.

Erickson also believed that the subconscious is responsible for most of our behaviors, and I certainly agree with this perspective, even if I generally go about addressing the issue from a different approach. Earlier I said I would teach you a 5-step hypnotic process. Unlike Erickson's approach, the process I will share is well defined, because I think it is good for those who are new to hypnosis to learn the fundamental steps involved in the hypnotic state. It will also utilize a far more directive or instructive therapeutic approach, because this is very practical for the majority of clients on our caseload.

Neuro-Linguistic Programming (or NLP) is often closely linked with hypnosis, and this is because the creators of NLP, John Grinder and Richard Bandler, when doing research on language patterns and searching for the secrets of successful therapists, discovered Erickson and studied the unique language patterns he commonly used during hypnosis sessions. By modeling his approaches they were able to replicate his successes, and thus incorporated methods of Ericksonian hypnosis into the structure and content of NLP.

Although the modalities taught in this book will primarily be directive, we will frequently discuss Ericksonian language patterns because they are interesting and effective. If you find the indirect approach helpful and useful to you, I encourage you to seek out further experience from an Ericksonian perspective. I also encourage you to take a course on neuro-linguistic programming. Unlike my co-author Nathan Thomas who is incredibly skilled at NLP, I personally don't call myself a neuro-linguistic programmer, but I have found the training interesting and beneficial to the therapeutic work I do.

Directive Hypnosis

Like Ericksonian hypnotherapy, the directive or traditional approach views trance as natural phenomena: I am not doing anything to you, I am merely facilitating the experiences that you already have. But while Ericksonian hypnosis is an indirect form utilizing conversational and metaphorical aspects in order to create trance and unconscious change, directive hypnosis or 'standard hypnosis' is primarily literal and straight forward.

Furthermore, direct hypnosis operates under the belief that the induction facilitates trance, and induction is therefore an essential element to the process. Both approaches have their uses. I have found that, especially with clients who have little or no prior experience with hypnosis, teaching them how to enter a deep level of trance is easily accomplished through the induction process. Now, if the client is already quite experienced and comfortable with hypnosis, then I may perhaps favor the Ericksonian approach; they'll come into the office and I'll simply say, "There is no need for an induction process today, just go right to where it is you'd like to be, and we'll go ahead and start the work." For the most part, however, it is my experience that most of our clients benefit from a formal induction process.

Another belief in traditional or directive hypnotherapy is that healing occurs as the result of shifting awareness, from the body to the thoughts, to mental images, to emotions. As hypnotists we need to tune into and shape our clients' awareness and experiences.

Direct hypnosis also teaches that the subconscious is extremely receptive to suggestion when in a state of trance. So, why not take advantage of this opportunity by making a specific, direct suggestion for positive change, rather than taking the chance of using a metaphor or stories that we hope our client grasps in the deeper interpretations they may conjure?

Calling Ericksonian hypnosis interactive does not mean that directive hypnosis is not interactive. The primary difference is that Erickson's approach is interactive during the actual hypnotic session, while the directive approach is more interactive before the session during the assessment interview. In directive hypnosis, the hypnotist is usually the only one talking during the trance state, imparting suggestions gleaned from prior conversation.

The Hypnotic Experience

I am now going to take you through a hypnotic experience. Yes, I am going to take you through the five-step hypnotic process right now while you are reading this book. This is how you really begin to learn how to hypnotize someone.

Please understand that this is just a building block, a brief demonstration, not a complete hypnosis session, but I want you to experience the process, and later on I will provide you with examples of me working with a client so that you can visualize doing the induction and deepening, and all the things that you will do with a live subject.

But for now I want you to actually experience a couple of moments of serenity. This will be rather rapid, but I promise that if you do this, even though you are sitting at home reading these pages and perhaps you might even feel a little bit funny, you will learn something new.

You must surely be wondering, is someone really going to hypnotize me using words on a page? Hypnosis is a natural process. It's a natural phenomenon. I'm simply going to guide you through a process of relaxation. It's going to be really simple. You will understand the process of hypnosis better as a result of this. The rest of the book will actually make much more sense to you as you learn the process of helping people to make changes. I'm going to take probably less than five minutes here and simply guide you through a rather brief process to help you experience the state of hypnosis.

Obviously, as you are reading there are many limitations, so what I would like you to do is to read through the following very carefully, maybe once or maybe twice to make sure it's all in your mind, and then I want you to follow the instructions, sit down, and experience hypnosis.

You may even want to have a friend read it to you, or as you read this just imagine yourself completing all the steps that the limitations of the written word will not allow you to. Following below is what I would say if I were hypnotizing you in person, so read it, and then once you are familiar with it remember it in your mind as you do it. By the way, if you find yourself slipping into a relaxed trance state even when just reading this, don't be surprised, it happens to a lot of people.

First, I would like you to find a comfortable place. Chances are you are already in a comfortable chair. By the way, I like it when people are in chairs when they first learn hypnosis. Later on we can take hypnosis to the bedroom and lie down, but I don't want my clients to fall asleep, so a chair is perfect.

Make sure you are comfortable and make sure your arms are at rest. Make sure your legs aren't crossed. While you are sitting there, what I would like you to do is simply stare at spot on the wall.

Just keep your eyes focused on that place. Take a deep breath. Breathe in... and exhale. Again, breathe in. Let the air fill your lungs and hold that breathe for a moment. Exhale.

Keep your eyes focused on that spot. As you keep your eyes focused on that area... I'd like you to begin to become aware of all the muscles in your body. Chances are pretty good that those muscles are carrying some of the tension of the day. Make a conscious effort to relax those muscles, the muscles in your shoulders, and your back, and your body.

Let your body become loose, limp as a pile of rubber bands. As you stare at that spot, you'll find that your eyes become perhaps more tired, maybe even a little bit watery.

As you stare at that spot, the next time your eyes blink, use that as a cue to simply close your eyes and keep them closed. If you haven't blinked yet, go ahead and blink your eyes. Use that as a cue to simply relax and close your eyes and keep them closed.

As you relax... as your eyes are closed... I'd like you to think of something beautiful that you find peaceful and relaxing. Take another breath. Feel the air slowly fill your lungs... and exhale. Allow yourself to go deeper into relaxation and hypnosis.

A part of you knows that you could open your eyes if you wanted to, but because you are letting yourself relax... and because it feels good... you simply don't care to open your eyes.

As you relax... as you enjoy a moment of tranquility... as in your mind's eye you look at the beautiful creation that you have envisioned... allow yourself to feel a perfect peace and relaxation.

Let your mind wonder. Let your thoughts experience positive things. In the quiet serenity that you are currently experiencing, just let yourself go deeper and deeper into a state of relaxation.

As you experience relaxation, peace and serenity, give yourself the gift of learning. Open your mind to new possibilities and to experience all of the things that we talk about in these pages and retain that knowledge... use that knowledge to benefit the clients on your caseload.

As you experience this moment of serenity, recognize that you can choose to go back to this place of peace at any time. Simply by making the decision to experience this state of tranquility that you've created in your mind.

I'm going to count from one to three. As I count from one to three, you will become more alert and more aware of the room around you.

One...you are becoming fully alert, reorienting to the room around you. Two...you are opening your eyes. You are feeling a sense of satisfaction. Three...total peace, total serenity, and total relaxation.

- - - - -

So now, go find a comfortable seat, re-read this, and simply allow yourself to be hypnotized. Once you have enjoyed that peaceful state for a few moments, just allow your eyes to open, feel good, and return to a normal state of mind ready to continue learning the wonders of hypnosis. Do not read any further in the text until you have done this, okay?

- - - - -

Now think: How long was that experience? Was it three, four, or five minutes long? Did you experience serenity for a couple of minutes? It was a complete hypnotic process, although abbreviated.

Many of you are probably thinking that you weren't hypnotized. You feel as if you were fully aware of everything that was going on. But in hypnosis, our subject *is* fully aware of everything that is going on.

Here are a couple questions to answer if you want to know whether you were hypnotized or not:

Number one, did you follow the directions that I gave you?

If you kept your focus on the spot and closed your eyes and you followed my suggestions and went through the process, then yes, you entered a state of trance.

Number two, after spending three or four or five minutes going through that process, do you feel different at the conclusion of the process? Do you feel physically more relaxed? Mentally, do you feel more receptive to learning? From an experiential perspective, did you find that was useful to you?

If the answer to any of those questions is yes, then you experienced a state of change. That state change could simply be called hypnosis. It could even be said you hypnotized yourself; you put the book down, and allowed it to work. You did it in your head, so in a way you have just hypnotized your first subject – yourself - haven't you?

Now, let us quickly dissect the demonstration in regards to the pre-talk, the induction, the deepener, the script, and the awakening.

Educating our client about hypnosis, the hypnotic process, and what the experience is going to be like is important, and therefore the pre-talk is the first component. A lot of new clients experience anxiety about hypnosis because they are not sure exactly what it is and they want to feel informed and comfortable before they give consent. So, in the pre-talk, I will spend some time talking about what hypnosis is and how it works, debunk any myths they may have, assure them that I will be respectful and that they won't be telling me secrets during the session, build a sense of trust and rapport, and allay any other concerns.

I gave a short pre-talk: I told you what to expect - that if you did what I asked you to do, you would feel great and you would be more effective at learning hypnosis.

The induction that I walked you through was a simple Eye Fixation combined with Muscle Relaxation. Fixating your gaze on one spot on the wall induces eye fatigue, and then I encouraged you to loosen all your muscles to let go of the tension of the day.

Admittedly, in this short demonstration I did not use a profound deepener, although I did suggest that you would go deeper into a state of hypnosis and experience deeper levels of relaxation, but I did not do what one might call a traditional deepener, simply for the sake of time.

Next, I gave you a few directive suggestions to feel good, that your learning process would be enhanced, and that you would benefit from this book.

And then after a moment of serenity, I concluded the session with a simple 3-count number awakening to show you how to return to a normal alert state of awareness.

The 'script' you read above was short, but it contained all the important components of facilitating the hypnotic process. When you begin hypnotizing others, you will use a similar formula or script, although when you move up to therapeutic sessions it will be much longer and more detailed.

And this is where a little bit of unease begins to creep into the minds of new hypnotists – what do I say? What if I mess up the words or the order or say something dumb? Should I memorize the induction and the suggestions, or can I write it all down first and read it from paper?

Let me set your mind at ease before we go any further. We do not have to be perfect in the language that we use. The most important factor is that we are genuine and that we assist our clients in experiencing hypnosis in a positive way.

A lot of people are hung up on the words they use; worried they might say the wrong thing. Unless you are disrespecting your clients or using aversion therapy or making suggestions that are unacceptable or conflict with what our clients would like to experience as their goals, there is really no danger in you saying the wrong thing.

If we mess up a word or two, it's okay. In regular conversation I don't always enunciate every word correctly, and neither do you. Every now and then we trip over or misstate a word, and it is okay if we are not flawless in our communication when facilitating an induction or giving suggestions. Sometimes when I'm writing on the board during a training workshop I misspell words because I'm busy trying to think and talk and teach and write. It's the same kind of thing - my students still understand exactly what I am trying to communicate whether I spell all the words correctly or not. Our clients are in a state of trance and will still understand what we want them to do, especially if they are a willing participant engaged in the learning process. They are not necessarily aware of a word or two that we missed; they are hearing the broader context.

The Elements of Hypnosis

As you read the following discourse about the elements of hypnosis, think about whether or not you feel you experienced them during the previous demonstration.

Hypnotic Voice / Tone

A significant element of the hypnotic process - which you were unable to experience in the traditional way through this medium, unless you had someone read the script to you - is the idea of a 'hypnotic voice.' If you listen to any self-hypnosis CDs or experience a live hypnosis session, you may notice that the hypnotist often speaks in a rather different and special tone of voice, one designed to convey confidence, calm, trust, and general serenity. This is important to the hypnotic process, and you will want to practice this voice to perfection.

You should speak clearly and loudly - not necessarily louder than normal conversation, but take care that you do not whisper or trail off at the end of words or sentences, or drop consonants (especially Ds and Ts). Also, take care not to speak too quickly, or too slowly.

It is good practice to regularly read aloud from a book or newspaper, and to open your mouth a little wider when you speak. Doing so, you may notice that the words are clearer and project a more confident sound.

You may wish to record yourself so that you know how your voice sounds to others (which is different than how it sounds to yourself), and practice using different tones until you are comfortable with both the quality and consistency.

Hypnotic Posture

The way you are seated, both the hypnotist's physical posture and the posture of the client, can be very important to the outcome of the hypnotic process.

Before I asked you to try the hypnosis demonstration, during the pre-talk phase, I said, *First, I would like you to find a comfortable place. Chances are you are already in a comfortable chair. By the way, I like it when people are in chairs when they first learn hypnosis. Later on we can take hypnosis to the bedroom and lie down, but I don't want my clients to fall asleep, so a chair is perfect. Make sure you are comfortable and make sure your arms are at rest. Make sure your legs aren't crossed.*

I believe it is important to get our clients in the correct posture to learn hypnosis. Those who do yoga may find the techniques useful for helping our clients to experience a hypnotic posture that is beneficial to relaxation and the learning process. For the most part, I want my clients comfortable in a chair with their arms to their side, with their legs uncrossed, taking a deep breath, and feeling the air fill their lungs. This helps prepare them for the process of relaxation. Relaxation is not essential to hypnosis, but it is certainly very useful.

As the hypnotist, posture is important to both your overall professional appearance and your hypnotic voice. If you look down while reading a script aloud and your chin is close to your chest, it will change the tonal quality of your voice.

Try speaking both ways, and notice the difference (record it if possible). Read a passage (from anything, but preferably a hypnosis script) aloud while looking down, and then, with your head level (eyes looking forward) and your neck straight - read it aloud again. You will notice that the sound of your voice is immediately clearer with your head raised, because the larynx is able to work unhindered.

Always try to keep your head level and your neck straight · when you speak, as this adds to the clarity and the innate sound of confidence and authority in your voice. Additionally, improved physical fitness not only helps develop posture and lung power, but also tends to 'sweeten' vocal harmonics.

Hypnotic Setting

I think a hypnotic setting is important. You may be reading this book in a variety of different places. I took for granted earlier that you were in a comfortable, quiet environment, but this may not have been true at all; you may have been reading on the subway or in a noisy office. Yet, can a client be hypnotized in a noisy bar? Absolutely – it can be accomplished. I have seen it done and I have done it myself.

People can be hypnotized in any environment, however in the therapeutic or clinical hypnosis process, if we have the opportunity to enhance hypnosis with a hypnotic setting, we should make the effort. Just as with traditional therapy, you want to present an attitude of professionalism with both your own appearance and the sur-roundings of the session. A comfortable chair should be available for the client, and you should be comfortable as well, whether sitting or standing. The room should be free of sight and sound distractions during the induction process. Dimming lights are a plus, and maybe decorate with a fish tank or relaxing images on the walls, comfortable furniture. All of these things can contribute positively to a hypnotic setting.

A Willing Subject

For hypnosis to work the subject being hypnotized must be willing to be hypnotized; they must want to listen and follow your suggestions. If you didn't do what I asked you to do in the previous demonstration, nothing will happen. By the way, that was kind of a profound statement - if our clients are not willing to do what we ask them to do, I can reasonably guarantee that nothing will change for them. However, when we have a willing subject, the hypnotic process is highly effective.

Unwilling, nervous, or skeptical clients may only need a more detailed pre-talk explanation of the process to answer any lingering questions or concerns. Should they be adamantly resistant, they may simply need to be referred for more traditional forms of therapy.

Confident Therapist

The additional characteristic we need is confidence. Are you confident that you can induce a hypnotic trance? It takes a bold person to get on stage in a noisy tavern and say, "Welcome to tonight's show! If you'd like to experience hypnosis, come on up here to the stage and become a star." Stage hypnotists must be very confident individuals.

I remember the first time I did a stage show: I was terrified! There is really no way to practice doing stage hypnosis, there simply is no way to grasp that experience until you are actually up on stage doing it. You can't just find 50 or 100 people and say that you want to try this out and see if this works; you have to get it right the very first time, and it takes a tremendous amount of confidence to do so.

Clinical hypnotists must also be bold and have confidence in themselves and the hypnotic process. For the client to trust you and be completely willing to follow your suggestions during the induction and the suggestive hypnotherapy session, they need to feel that they are in competent hands, so you must present yourself as being totally sure about what you are doing - even at first when you are new and inexperienced.

This is both an attitude and a natural skill that will come from practice. The only real way to practice hypnosis is to do it, so once you've practiced a million times in your head, you essentially have to 'fake it until you make it,' cross your fingers, hold your breath and just go for it.

Knowledge of Approaches

Another important element is knowledge of various hypnotic approaches to inducing and deepening hypnosis, and being able to determine (through assessment) which approaches will be more beneficial to the individual client. This knowledge comes from research and practice, along with a healthy dose of common sense.

In the previous brief demonstration, I used an eye fixation and relaxation induction. We will talk in more detail about different methods of induction later (Elman number count, Speed Trance, arm levitation, fractionation, etc), but for now just know that it is important for you to develop a broad repertoire of techniques, because different clients will respond better (or worse) to different styles and approaches.

For example, clients who have never been hypnotized before can be very anxious and apprehensive about the process. Sometimes in this circumstance I will use an awareness induction to help ease them into trance, by guiding the client into experiencing and becoming aware of what their body is doing.

Just as some people like flashy clothes and others are more subdued, and some like rock and roll music and others prefer country and western, some clients like to feel the hypnotic process physically or even see it visually, while others like to metaphorically drift, dream and float. If you try to fit every client into the same generic induction and deepening mold, the hypnosis may not effective.

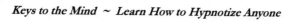

Hypnotic Myth-Busting

Now would be a good time to talk about some of the myths associated with hypnosis. During the initial intake or assessment process with a new client, we need to discover if they have ever been hypnotized before, and if not, we need an idea of what they know or think about hypnosis. Perhaps they have listened to a hypnosis or relaxation CD, or have seen a stage hypnotist at a county fair, or maybe all they know is that their neighbor somehow quit smoking with hypnosis, whatever that is, and they want to quit too. Clients often call to schedule a hypnosis appointment because they have heard it can be beneficial to them, but they don't know exactly what hypnosis is, and consequently while they desire the benefits, they may still be fearful of the unknown process.

When we understand the many myths that people believe about hypnosis, we can address them during the assessment process and the pre-talk. In order to be effective at hypnosis, you need to know the truth so you will have answers for your clients and be able to counter their misconceptions.

Hypnosis Demonstrations are Bad

The first myth, interestingly enough, is that stage hypnosis, or hypnosis for entertainment or any use outside of clinical care, is bad. Some professional associations like to espouse that no one but an MD or a psychologist should be allowed to practice hypnosis, and they are entitled to their position and attempt to project themselves as the only qualified experts in the field of hypnosis. However, in reality, a lot of non-medical people practice hypnosis, and many of those folks are stage performers.

The fact is, hypnotic phenomena can be quite entertaining, and the stage performer simply manifests or demonstrates natural hypnotic phenomena with a group of individuals. Watching your friend temporarily forget her own name or the number two is funny. Seeing people acting silly on stage playing a musical instrument that doesn't really exist is an amusing thing to witness.

Demonstrating hypnotic phenomena does not harm the subject. As a matter of fact, those who say that hypnosis should never be used for entertainment probably should not watch any of Milton Erickson's training videos, because Milton Erickson loved to play with his patients. Many of his videos from the 1960's and 70's were powerful demonstrations of physical and verbal hypnotic phenomena, because Erickson himself found it entertaining as well as educational. Furthermore, many psychology professors demonstrate hypnotic phenomena in their classrooms, not only because it shows how powerful hypnosis really is, but also because it's an entertaining thing to do in a hum-drum class.

Personally, I think saying that a person should not be allowed to demonstrate hypnotic phenomena on stage (or anywhere outside a clinical office) is a lot like saying a person can't make a movie that is depressing because depression is real, or that we shouldn't be able to make a TV show that is happy because happiness is real.

Demonstrating hypnotic phenomenon on stage is actually a good thing for the profession overall, because as you will soon discover, before most clients call our office for an appointment, their only experience with hypnosis was either via word of mouth or through witnessing a stage show.

When someone sees a stage hypnotist perform, they generally leave believing three things: One, that hypnotism is fun; two that hypnotism made people feel good, and three that hypnotism is powerful – it really works.

Now, there are some bad stage hypnotists out there, just like there are bad psychologists and social workers. Sometimes people go to a traditional therapy session and leave feeling miserable, and this can of course happen at a stage hypnosis show too, or at a comedy show or a magic show or a rock concert. People can have bad experiences anywhere, and some people just like to have a bad time. On the whole, however, people leave a stage hypnosis show happily in awe, and this positive exposure is good for driving referrals to the clinical profession.

Hypnosis is an Altered State of Consciousness

The second myth that people often believe is that hypnosis is a (negatively) altered state of consciousness. An "altered state" implies an external factor contributing to a change, such as drunkenness or being stoned on drugs. Hypnosis, as previously discussed, is a natural state that we all enter a few times each day. Researchers have divided our natural brain functions into four separate levels of cycles per second, or CPS.

(CPS) Activity Levels:

1. BETA
   Normal daytime consciousness, critical thought level. (18 - 40 CPS)

2. ALPHA
   Relaxation level - beginning to awaken in the morning and crossing over into sleep at night. Associated with imaginative thinking; corresponds to light and medium levels of Hypnosis. (8 - 18 CPS)

3. THETA
   Early stages of sleep; deep daydreaming state. Associated with creative thinking; corresponds to medium and deep levels of Hypnosis. (4 - 7 CPS)

4. DELTA
   Profound sleep; dream state. (1 - 3 CPS)

That's it; there's no place else for your brain to go, during hypnosis or otherwise. For most people, hypnosis is a mid-*alpha* range activity, and although you are under hypnosis, you remain fully conscious of everything that is going on.

Hypnosis is simply a matter of setting aside the conscious mind, to one degree or another, and selectively focusing one's attention on either a particular point or a whole range of experiences.

Because of the hyper suggestibility inherent in the *alpha* and *theta* levels, positive programming during hypnosis is extremely effective in helping to create positive life changes.

Our brains function all day long between the highest level (the *beta* level) and the lowest level of brain wave functioning (the *delta* level). At *beta* level, between 18 and 40 cycles per second, our brain is at a fully alert stage. If you are driving in rush hour traffic or you are looking at a map trying to find a new route home, chances are pretty good you are functioning in the highest levels of *beta* brain wave activity. This is typical daytime alertness; we are consciously aware of the things around us and we are making cognitive decisions about actions and people and the things.

Early in the morning when we first get up, when we are crossing over into sleep at night, and even maybe around two or three o'clock in the afternoon after a long lunch, we are likely to be at the *alpha* level of brain wave functioning, between 8 and 18 cycles per second. At this level, we are awake but relaxed. This is the stage where imaginative thinking or daydreaming occurs, and it corresponds to light and medium levels of trance.

The *theta* level of brain wave functioning, at 4 to 7 cycles per second, is a profound state of deep trance. *Theta* is associated with the early stages of sleep and sometimes with deeper daydreams, and corresponds with creative thinking and medium to deep levels of hypnosis.

The deepest level of brain wave functioning is the *delta* level, 1 to 3 cycles per second. At about four o'clock in the morning, you're in the delta level, a state of deep and profound sleep.

No matter the time of day or night, we are functioning between natural *beta* and *delta* levels; we can't go anywhere else.

Hypnotized Subjects are Asleep

The third common myth regarding hypnosis is that the subject is asleep. Hypnosis comes from the Greek word *hypnos,* which literally translates to sleep, however this name is inaccurate. Hypnosis is generally a profound state of relaxation, a lowered state of brain level functioning and activity where our subconscious mind is more attuned and open to new ideas, but it is different from sleep; a sleeping person cannot usually respond to suggestion.

If you use the word sleep with your clients, let them know, especially during the induction, that this is not like night time sleep, this is sleep like relaxation and letting go of the tension of the day.

Hypnosis Conflicts with Religion

The fourth myth, which ties in closely with the fifth, is that hypnosis violates religious rules. I was chatting with a friend who is a massage therapist and asked her, "Hey, do you and your husband ever use hypnosis at your massage therapy clinic?" Her eyes grew wide and she stammered, "Oh no. We would never do that." Curious about her response, I asked, "Why not?" She said, "No, no. Hypnosis violates our religion."

Instead of getting into a debate, I just accepted her answer and moved on. There are a lot of people out there who believe there is a religious prohibition against hypnosis, and I think this comes primarily from the myths or misconceptions that people have about hypnosis, such as hypnosis is a door-way to the devil or akin to mind control.

Hypnosis is a Form of Mind Control

This brings us to the fifth myth, that a hypnotized person subjects their mind or gives their will over to the control of another person. This is not true. The Svengali-esq mystical, all-powerful quality attached to hypnosis originally came about from the 1894 novel *Trilby*, by George Du Maurier, which interestingly enough has been called the first 'Best Seller.' Du Maurier died two years later but his characters, the evil stage hypnotist Svengali and his abused love Trilby, still live on today, having been recreated by Hollywood an impressive twelve times between 1896 and 1983, and the book was republished again in 1994.

Admittedly, some stage hypnotists like to be perceived as having magical powers because it makes for good showmanship; that is their chosen performance persona, their stage presence approach, even though it is not a scientific reality. Again, hypnosis is a proven safe, natural and effective process that harnesses natural abilities, God-given abilities, if you believe that way, which already reside within us. And because of this fact, I cannot think of any religion that wouldn't want us to use our mind to the highest level of potential, or any religion that has a belief system contra-indicated by hypnotic process.

The only reason a person would believe that religious rules prohibit hypnosis is because they have a misunderstanding about the true nature of hypnosis; they believe it to be an altered state of consciousness, or perhaps a form of meditation that is opposed to their accepted form of meditation, when others would say that hypnosis is really the opposite of meditation. Personally, my theory is that if the devil can climb inside a person's mind that easily, he probably doesn't need a hypnotic process to do so. However, the reality of Christian ideology is an entirely separate debate, and one which we will now leave to dinner parties and theologians.

A hypnotized person does not yield control and does not do anything in a hypnotic state that they would be opposed to doing in a waking state. Certainly people are more suggestible to ideas and new behaviors that are based on truth, but they are not suggestible to the point that they will violate their personal moral beliefs or the rules of society. The CIA and the KGB spent a lot of time and money in the 1950's and 60's trying to figure out how to use hypnosis to create the perfect drone, the human without a conscience. Obviously, had they succeeded, our world would likely be a far different place.

The original *Manchurian Candidate* movie with Frank Sinatra in 1963, however, had better success and was able to use hypnosis to create the perfect drone Presidential assassin. Hollywood likes to play the mind-control card because it makes good theater, but the reality is people maintain total control during hypnosis, always possessing the ability to accept or reject any suggestions they receive from the hypnotist. Hypnosis is simply a lot more interesting and entertaining when portrayed as something sinister or comedic. Likewise, the average soccer mom driving her sedan down a city street is rather boring to witness when compared to a high-speed Maserati-driving drug-dealer police chase on the freeway.

Further proof about the lack of mind-control can actually be found at the occasional bad stage hypnosis show. People like to have fun and feel good, and when a hypnotist begins to disrespect the subjects or give negative suggestions, they will be rejected. I attended a show at a comedy club once and it was pretty good – the subjects were quite responsive and everyone was having a good time – until about half way through the show. I don't know what happened, but the hypnotist's mood changed or maybe he decided on the spot to experiment a bit, and it all went downhill from there.

He was giving post-hypnotic suggestions with keywords, and unlike the tone of the previous skits, these were all negative. For example, he actually said, "The person I am touching now, when I say the word Blue, you will feel as if someone has kicked you in the balls." And then, moving on to the next person, he actually said, "The person I'm touching now, when I say the word Candida, you will feel as if someone has goosed you, you know, poked their finger right up in your ass hole and gave it a good twist." (Yes, he really said this.)

As a general rule, when keywords are used like this in a stage show they are attached to humorous behaviors, like, "Any time I say the color Blue, you will jump up and sing *Blue Suede Shoes* and dance like Elvis." Most anyone can and would happily respond to this silly suggestion, but no one likes to feel as if they've been blind-sided with a kick in the groin, or elsewhere.

This hypnotist went on to give seven subjects seven different keywords, all with these kinds of terribly negative suggestions. Let me just state again that this was not a good show! Who would want to experience those kinds of things? Where is the humor in this? Even members of the audience were taken aback. These people volunteered to go up on stage because they were told it was going to be fun and they would feel good, but now the hypnotist is handing out non-pleasurable, non-amusing suggestions. Unlike the first 20 or 30 minutes of the show when things were going well and everyone was laughing and having a great time, the subjects now appeared a little confused and nervous, likely wondering if they could still trust the hypnotist. Not good.

He then went on with his patter or script where he uses the keywords and the subject responds accordingly. He said, "Well, I went outside my hotel today and boy was it pretty out! I looked up at the clear blue sky..." And the blue keyword subject just sat there. He didn't respond. The hypnotist was clearly a little surprised, so he moved on to the next keyword, "So I was talking to my friend Candida... and Candida said..." Again, there was no response from the selected subject, and now the hypnotist was even more rattled. He quickly went through all seven of his keywords and only one out of the seven participants responded, but without much excitement.

Obviously relieved to be done with that part of the act, the hypnotist then went into a deepening skit and came back with more typical types of silly skits, but the subjects never again responded quite as enthusiastically as they had during the beginning of the show.

So again, when we are hypnotized, we do not yield control to another person, we simply become more suggestible in regards to accepting true and beneficial patterns of thinking.

You Can Become Stuck in Hypnosis

One of the greatest examples of the sixth myth is displayed in the 1999 movie, *Office Space*. If you haven't seen it, go rent it. It's a really funny film even with all the false stuff about hypnosis. In the movie, the main character, Peter Gibbins, is convinced by his girlfriend to go see a hypnotist, and while he's in trance receiving suggestions to relax, let go, not worry so much, the hypnotist has a heart attack and dies. Peter is then allegedly stuck in a state of hypnosis for most of the remainder of the movie, happily living quite laissez-faire, and laughter ensues.

If a hypnotherapist died in the middle of a session (or if the power was cut when listening to a self-hypnosis CD), one of two things would happen: one, the client would stop hearing the hypnotic voice and become more alert and wake up, or two, they would enter a deeper level of trance and eventually fall into natural sleep, waking naturally when they were rested. These are the only two things that can happen to a person who is hypnotized; they will either wake up or they will fall asleep. Remember, our brains are always working at one of four levels of functioning: *beta, alpha, theta* or *delta*.

Only Some People Can Be Hypnotized

This is simply untrue. Anyone and everyone *can* be hypnotized. Perhaps at a comedy stage hypnosis show only 20 out of 100 are willing to go up on stage, and maybe only 17 of those 20 will relax and trust the process enough to enter a qualifying trance, but the reality is that everyone *can* be hypnotized. Okay, there may be a few situational exceptions; I suppose drunk or drugged people, or perhaps those whose mental deficits prevent concentration, relaxation or the following of directions might not be easily hypnotizable.

Everyone has the ability to enter a different state of brainwave functioning – just as they do on a regular basis in their daily lives, driving a car, watching a movie, going to church, doing whatever it is that people do. It is true that some people choose not to be hypnotized in certain settings because their anxiety levels are too high. Usually this means that we haven't done an adequate pre-talk to educate them about hypnosis and help them overcome their fears. Some people are also more responsive to one style of induction over another, but a lot of this is dependent on their mood at the time, which can be assessed and targeted during the interview phase.

Stupid People are Easier to Hypnotize

A common misconception is that weak or less intelligent minds are easier to hypnotize. In reality, it is far easier to hypnotize people who have the ability to concentrate and focus and learn new things. The smarter you are, the easier it is to concentrate, and the harder you fall. Ask any stage performer and they will tell you they prefer doing college shows to any other form of stage hypnosis. Why? College students are smart; they had to be smart enough to get into college, their minds are young and active and they are accustomed to studying and following directions.

Hypnosis is Considered a 'New Age' or 'Alternative' Therapy

People often think of hypnosis as 'new age,' but it has been around for centuries. Egyptian hieroglyphics record use of hypnosis, and Greek sleep temples used hypnosis for healing.

Perhaps because the field is still not legally regulated in most US states, unlicensed practitioners - who may also be drawn to other unregulated or alternative healing methods - tend to learn and practice hypnosis at a greater rate than the rest of the population, but hypnosis in and of itself is not part of any new age movement or alternative therapy scheme.

Remember, the most prominent medical and psychological professional associations are not exactly the most liberal and accepting groups when it comes to alternative therapies, yet they all do formally accept hypnosis.

And the terms, "New Age" and "alternative therapy" aren't really useful terms; they are generally used negatively by one group in power to describe something that is either unprofitable to them, cuts into their base of power of finances, or something they have not take the time to understand.

Suggestibility is Fake

If you really believe that suggestibility isn't real or doesn't work, just ask any advertising executive and then stand back. You won't want to be hit when they double over laughing. How many items have you bought something you really didn't need "on impulse" at the check-out counter? Have you ever yawned after seeing the visual cue of someone else yawning first? History is replete with people responding to suggestion - often in mass - sometimes in healthy ways and sometimes in negative ways. How about right now, do you feel like stretching and yawning?

Hypnosis is the Best Treatment for Everything

This myth is a little different. Some people believe that hypnosis is always the best way to solve all problems, but this is not true; the best solution to a problem will obviously depend on what the problem is and the unique needs of the individual.

Different people respond better or worse to different approaches, depending on the issue at hand. For example, in my career as a drug and alcohol counselor I have used nicotine replacement therapy, methadone replacement therapy, 12-Step programs, behavioral self-control training and many other treatment approaches. Hypnosis is extremely effective at impacting many issues and conditions, but it is not the be-all and end-all of therapy. The effective hypnotist should be aware of many different approaches, and be willing to refer if the better choice is outside the scope of their practice abilities.

Hypnosis is *a* way to solve some problems. There is more than one way to skin a cat, and there is more than one way to quit smoking. Hypnosis, as with any other form of treatment, works for those whom it works for.

Trance Depth Must Be Certain

Another common erroneous belief is that trance depth is important. I have met many hypnotists who believe it is essential that their clients go into profound states of trance before they will begin suggestive work. In reality, the subconscious mind will do its work at any stage or level of trance.

At the conclusion of a session a client once said to me, "You know, I felt really relaxed, but I was aware of everything you said and everything that was going on." I then asked him how long the session was, and he said, "Pretty short this time, only about ten minutes." The session had actually been about a half-hour long. Time distortion. I then asked him about some of the things I suggested, but he was unable to answer my questions with any detail, because in reality, he had been in a much deeper level of trance than he even imagined possible.

I want my clients to be relaxed and feel good, to let go of their problems and leave them 1000 miles away. Trance depth is unimportant in clinical therapy. Our clients, even in the lightest levels of trance, will be able to learn new skills and benefit from hypnosis. We should not get hung up on aiming for trance depth, but instead simply focus on teaching our clients new skills and how to apply them to problem-solving in life.

Audio CDs are Not Real Hypnosis

The final myth is that recorded hypnosis, like sessions on a tape or CD, is not real hypnosis. As a matter of fact, the Journal of Gastroenterology found that when treating irritable bowel syndrome, clients responded equally as well to recorded hypnosis sessions as they did to live sessions.

For the hypnotic process to work, what is important is whether or not the client follows the directions that are given. If they do, they will experience trance and learn new skills, and their subconscious will be supplied with new information with which they can take new actions. If they do not follow directions, these things will not happen, whether they were listening to Memorex or a live hypnotist.

Live hypnosis does have key advantages however, such as the ability to be interactive when appropriate and adjust your suggestions based on client observation and feedback. A recording can ask questions for the client to ponder, but a virtual hypnotist cannot help make their answers more productive with additional or alternative targeted suggestions.

The History of Hypnosis

The foundations and the history of hypnosis are both fascinating and extremely important for helping us to truly understand the origins and nature of our craft, but don't worry, we won't spend too much time here, as I am sure you are eager to begin practicing hypnotic skills.

First and foremost we need to understand that hypnosis is not new; it has been used since the earliest records of mankind for healing, albeit by a different name. Some even claim that hypnosis was actually used at the beginning of time. The *Nelson Study Bible* states in Genesis 2:21: "And the Lord God caused a deep sleep to fall on Adam and he slept; and He took one of his ribs, and closed up the flesh in its place." I'm not getting into religion, but I do find it interesting that one of the first stories recorded in the bible is a story that seems to have the description of hypnosis being used as an anesthetic during surgery. We of course cannot know if that really is or is not the case, but it is certainly a curious concept to consider.

We do know for a fact, however, that early Greek and Egyptian civilizations used hypnotic trance-like sleep states for healing. They built what were called Sleep Temples, with hieroglyphics on the walls depicting doctor-like figures standing over what appear to be sleeping or tranced individuals during a healing process.

In the 1500's, the Middle Ages, the prevailing opinion was that disease was caused by evil spirits or by doing bad things. In response, priests and mystics used hypnosis for healing by putting people into a trance-like state and using hypnosis to rid people of the various conditions with which they were afflicted as a result of their sinful behavior. Today we might call this an exorcism.

We move into a more scientific era of hypnosis at about 1785. **Franz Anton Mesmer**, who is of course the origin of the words mesmerize and mesmerism, was clearly a significant player in terms of the history of hypnosis. Mesmer believed that there is magnetism in all things and all people, and that the flow of this magnetism, when interrupted, causes all illness.

As a treatment, he had his patients relax while he hovered his hands or waved magnetic rods over them. After several minutes of passes, he declared them cured. Before long his fame spread to a phenomenal degree, and he was curing up to 3000 patients per day, until eventually Benjamin Franklin was called in by the King of France to investigate and declared his work to be nothing more than "imagination," or in other words: the placebo effect.

But consider the placebo effect - it's a lot like hypnosis, isn't it? And even if there was no truth in Mesmer's theory of animal magnetism, what he did (simply a different way of inducing trance) worked for some reason, and even after being so-called debunked by Franklin, he still had many followers.

Two believers who piggybacked on Mesmer's work and understanding of trance and applied it in a different way were physicians **James Esdaile** and **James Braid**. Esdaile, who lived in British India in the 1800's, recorded doing over 340 invasive surgical procedures using an adaptation of mesmerism or hypnosis as an anesthetic.

Moving on to 1841, James Braid also performed surgeries using hypnosis. Braid is not only considered the "Father of Modern Hypnosis," but was also the first "hypnotherapist," credited with carefully choosing and then popularizing the word hypnosis, which as mentioned previously is derived from the Greek word *hypnos*, referring to the god of sleep.

Mesmer may be regarded as the grandfather of hypnosis, but Braid is the one who recognized the meaning and power of the hypnotic state, side-stepped around animal magnetism and the bad publicity of 'mesmerism,' ignored the imagination set, and advanced research tremendously along the psycho-physiological path, leading us towards today's form of hypnosis and hypnotherapeutic practice.

Thanks to Braid, by the 1880's, many physicians were performing great work and research in the area of medical and psychological hypnosis. For example, in 1884, **Ambroise Liébeault** emphasized how hypnosis was a natural phenomenon induced by the power of suggestion. His ideas founded the Nancy School (or Suggestive School) of thought regarding hypnosis, where Émile Coué and Sigmund Freud came to observe and study. Liébeault is considered the "Father of Modern Hypnotherapy."

From 1914 to 1918 during World War I, chemical anesthesia had not yet come into play but the Germans used hypnosis on the battlefield for analgesic needs, pain management and surgical procedures, and as a psychiatric treatment. One of the first recorded uses of hypnosis for treatment of psychiatric disorders was by the Germans for what was then called shell-shock syndrome.

We move now into the early to mid-1900's, with **Milton Erickson** and **Émile Coué**, two gentlemen who have probably had the greatest influence on our generation's version of modern hypnotism. Milton Erickson came up with the hypothesis that not only is hypnosis is a naturally occurring phenomenon, but therefore formal inductive procedures are not necessary in order to produce trance or therapeutic benefits or to help people make changes.

As mentioned before, Erickson's method of psychotherapy involves using conversational hypnotic language in order to induce trance in individuals. He would start his sessions by talking about the everyday experiences that clients have. This conversational approach predicates hypnotic intervention on the client's frame of reference, and this model of therapy is adhered to by most practitioners who use hypnotherapy professionally today.

In the early 1900's, Émile Coué was, in my mind at least, the "Father of Positive Thinking." He believed that repeating words or images enough times will cause the subconscious to absorb them, and subsequently he developed a mantra-like conscious auto-suggestion, "Every day, in every way, I'm getting better and better."

Dave Elman is another hypnotic pioneer who operated at the same time as Milton Erickson (1950's-60's). Elman pioneered many rapid and directive uses of hypnotic trance and created the famous 'Elman Induction,' a 3-minute hypnotic induction still used frequently today.

This brief discourse from page 57 of *Findings in Hypnosis* should give you a good idea of Dave Elman's fundamental philosophy: "The ways of inducting hypnosis are almost countless. And while some methods take longer than others, they can all be used to produce the deep state known as somnambulism... The methods of achieving the trance state are limited only by your own imagination.

There is no way in which you cannot hypnotize a patient, provided you know the art of suggestion... Since eye-closure is the first goal at which you must aim, all you need is a device that will cause it. *Any* device will cause it, provided you know the art of suggestion and provided the person expects to be hypnotized... This applies even to patients who have never been previously conditioned."

Three Laws of Suggestion

Émile Coué also came up with what I refer to as the Three Laws of Suggestion. These provide a foundation for most of the suggestive therapy that we will use with the clients on our caseload today.

The Law of Concentrated Attention

Whenever attention is concentrated on an idea over and over again, it spontaneously tends to realize itself, provided the idea is within the realms of possibility. Coué's focus was on aiding the effects of medications for medical conditions, and he believed that if a patient believed that the medicine would work and they would be cured, and focused their attention on being cured, they would indeed become cured. This approach was amazingly effective.

The Law of Reverse Effort

Coué believed that the harder one *tries* to do something, the less chance they have for success. A perfect example is when you really need a good night's sleep, and you know the alarm is going to go off at six o'clock in the morning, so you go to bed at ten o'clock instead of eleven o'clock because you know you need to sleep. You try to make yourself sleep, and now it's eleven o'clock. You're flopping around on the bed trying to get comfortable, trying to sleep, and at midnight you're still rolling around. At two-thirty in the morning, you've had it! You're at the point where you're looking at the clock saying, "Okay, if I go to sleep now, I'll have three hours and forty-one minutes of sleep." And then a while later it's, "If I finally get to sleep now, I'll never be able to wake up, so I'd better just get up now and stay awake." This is the law of reverse effort in action.

The more someone tries to quit smoking, the more they smoke. The more you try to remember something, the harder it is to remember. Coué's idea was to focus less on the willpower and more on the imagination for greater results, and to replace negative thoughts with positive ones. For example, don't stress and say, "I'll never remember the combination to that lock!" Instead, say, "Oh well, it will come to me in a few minutes," and most likely it will.

The Law of Dominant Effect

The law of dominant effect means that a strong emotional suggestion tends to replace a weaker one. The more emotionally intense or relevant a concept is, the more likely it is to take hold and be followed.

Émile Coué was a very important and valued contributor to our early understanding of hypnosis, and we will rely heavily on the principles of his three laws of suggestion as we structure our hypnotic suggestions.

CHAPTER 3

The Mechanics of the Hypnotic Process ~ How to Hypnotize Anyone

This is it, what you've been waiting for: You are about to learn the mechanics of hypnosis, how to actually work through the hypnotic process and induce trance in someone.

We will spend some time talking about the fundamental steps involved in pre-talk and assessment, induction and deepening techniques, pre-scripted suggestive scripts, and awakening or de-hypnotizing our client. If you follow this process, you will indeed be able to hypnotize anyone.

However, there is more to hypnotherapy than simply being able to put someone into a trance like state, and we will discuss these things as well along the way.

The Pre-Talk

Before we actually begin an inductive process, a pre-talk is essential. If you go see a stage performance, during the first five or so minutes before the hypnotist invites volunteers up to the stage he or she will give an introduction and the pre-talk. When a client comes to you for a hypnotherapy appointment, they won't come in, sit in the recliner and instantly be inducted. Instead, you will first to spend a little bit of time with the client performing an assessment interview as part of the pre-talk.

During the pre-talk, we will find out whether or not our client been hypnotized before, and if so, what their experience was like. We will build rapport by matching and mirroring their body language and patterns of speech, and just generally being nice and friendly. We will then ask if they have any specific questions for us. Sometimes our clients have questions for us about hypnosis that we've never even thought about before, so it is important to ask not only because it overcomes resistance, but also because on many occasions we can learn something from our clients. They may have fears and anxieties about hypnosis which are logically absurd, but ignorance is simply an absence of knowledge, so it is our job to be patient and gently lead them to a place of understanding and acceptance through education and answering questions.

I let clients know that even though I might use the word sleep they will not actually be asleep; sleep in this context is just another word for a trance-like state. And, depending on the response I receive, I may also define the word trance. *Trance is a natural occurring phenomenon and a state of being that we all experience every day, much like highway hypnosis. It's a condition of profound relaxation. Like when you're driving a car and ...* I let my clients know, "You can't stay hypnotized. I can't get you to do anything against your will, and you will always be safe and can emerge at anytime you choose," and so forth.

The pre-talk also builds trust. Our clients are essentially going to be sleeping with us for the next 30 minutes or so, if you'll excuse the phrase, and so they want to know the person with whom they will be sleeping. Clients need to feel they can trust me, to know that Richard really is a nice guy who wants to help them out. Building trust is essential during the pre-talk, because if we don't have the client's trust we will not build a therapeutic relationship, which means it is unlikely they will go into a trance state and enjoy the benefits of hypnosis.

I always let my clients know during the pre-talk that there are four things I can promise them:

Number one is that they are going to feel better than they have ever felt before if they participate in today's session.

Number two is that all hypnosis is self-hypnosis. I am not going to be doing anything *to* them, but I am going to be guiding them through a process of hypnosis that their bodies already know how to participate in.

Number three is that hypnosis will in fact help them with the issues that they have presented today.

And number four, I always assure my clients that while we are engaged in the process of hypnosis I will never ask them to do anything humiliating nor to reveal any secrets to me that are not part of the presenting problem and the therapeutic process. I'll tell them right up front that I respect what is important to them; their privacy and their dignity.

All of these things are important to communicate during the pre-talk and assessment interview session.

Convincers

Convincers are another hallmark of the pre-talk, particularly with new clients, as they help to break the ice and let people know what hypnosis is really all about, through demonstrations or examples of waking hypnosis. This helps clients learn the process of following suggestions, and helps us to measure resistance and self-development. If we do a couple of convincers during the pre-talk phase and the client is not responding appropriately, then maybe we need to go back and address more their potential myths or fears, to discover how or why this person come in with the idea of challenging the hypnotist, or whatever their resistance issue may be.

One of the most popular convincers frequently used by both stage hypnotists and clinical hypnotherapists is the simple "Fingers Drawn Together" test.:

> "Hold your arms straight out in front of you, with your fingers clasped together, and then extend the pointer or index finger of each hand.
>
> Now, pull those two fingers apart as far as possible, and stare hard at the space between them.
>
> As you stare between your fingers a magnetic force begins to pull your fingers together.
>
> You will notice that no matter how hard you try to keep your fingers apart, they are being drawn closer and closer together. The harder you pull, the stronger the magnet becomes and pulls them together.
>
> Focus on the space between your fingers. Pull harder. Can you feel the magnet? Your fingers are being drawn by the magnet, closer and closer together, until they touch."

Now, if a client's fingers do not close, that is fine too. We simply tell them *this shows they have the ability to focus and concentrate. There really isn't a right or wrong answer here; if they have the ability to resist the magnetic pull they feel between their fingers, they are focusing, but not focusing on the point between those two fingers as I have instructed.* I'll educate them on following instructions or try a different convincer, taking the time to further build rapport and trust.

Clients can feel a little silly or embarrassed at first with their fingers up in the air, so maintaining a positive, encouraging demeanor and moving on to another convincer - no matter their initial success or failure - can help them to relax and in the groove of following instructions and going with the process.

Another ice-breaking convincer is the "Circle and the 6"

"Sit up straight in your chair with your feet flat on the floor.

Which hand do you write with?" (Left or right?)

"Good. Now, raise that arm and point up (at a slight angle, like to a far corner of the room - demonstrate), and extend and raise your (right/left) foot off the ground (foot from same side as arm - left/left or right/right).

Excellent. Now, I want you to do two things at the same time.

With your finger, you're going write the number 6 in the air, starting at the top (counter-clockwise, demonstrate) - and - with your foot, you're going to make a clockwise circle (demonstrate)."

NOTE: You will demonstrate these two actions separately. Why? Because as the client will instantly discover when they try it, it's darn near impossible to do them both at the same time, at least without highly concentrated practice.

Now, you try.

After the inevitable laughter, continue:

"Now, try it again, but draw the 6 from the loop up, while moving your foot (both clockwise, demonstrate) - or from the top down, but change direction of your foot (both counter-clockwise, demonstrate)."

-- And then you might briefly discuss left/right brain functioning and concentration, because it's interesting.

As I once heard a stage hypnotist say, "This doesn't have a whole lot to do with hypnosis, but it is just darned cool." Actually, it does have a lot to do with hypnosis: it shows our client's willingness to follow suggestions, the difference between left and right brain thinking, the importance of concentration, and of simply looking at things from a new and unique or different perspective. Even though it's not really considered a classic conditioning convincer, it's one I like because people simply have fun doing those sorts of things – and it's one they will remember and share with others.

As the client enters a trance state they begin to exhibit hypnotic phenomena, and pointing these occurrences out helps by convincing or encouraging them to relax even further. Erickson used to do this all the time; he'd be talking with the client and simply say something like, 'and are you aware that your breathing has begun to slow down... Your eyelids seem to flutter as you listen to me...' This is an extremely powerful way of beginning to get your clients comfortable with the idea of going into hypnosis.

The pre-talk, including convincers, sets the stage for the future work we will do with the client. Ormund McGill has been referred to as the Dean of American Hypnosis. In his book, *The New Encyclopedia of Stage Hypnotism*, he describes four principles of a good convincer, and these four things are important to incorporate into our pre-talk.

Four Principles of a Good Convincer:

1. **We must lock our client's mind on the specific suggestion we have given.**

2. **To have a person lock their mind around an idea, the suggestion must be given with confidence.**

3. **Presentation must be made in a way that does not bring the critical factors of the mind into action.** (This is where experience and hypnotic language are important.)

4. **The client must be free from objection, so they will want to experience the suggestion.**

We must tell the client with confidence and certainty that their *hands are locked together, and even though they know they could pull them apart, at this moment they now feel like they cannot. Their hands become tighter and tighter and tighter and it is now impossible for them to pull their hands apart* - even though all rational thought would tell them that it is possible. *The harder they try to pull their hands apart, the more difficult it becomes and their hands have become completely and totally locked together....*

We have to lock our client's mind on the convincer, and we accomplish this by giving suggestions at the client's individual level of functioning, so that we can avoid them entering back into the critical factor of reasoning and failing at the convincer that we're giving them. Simply put, this process makes make sure our clients understand what we are saying - without them having to really think about it.

Then, of course, probably the most important aspect of a convincer is that our client must be willing to participate, to actually do what we suggest they do. If the client is unwilling to follow along with our instructions, they will not benefit from hypnotherapy.

The Induction

Once we have spent time with a client in the pre-talk and convincer stage, we can then move on to the induction. Our client has come to us for help to resolve their issue; they want to feel better than they have ever felt before. We have overcome some of their fears and anxieties by building a relationship with them and explaining a little bit about the hypnosis process to them, and now we can go ahead with an induction.

The formal induction of hypnosis does not need to be a long process. With clients who have been hypnotized before, a two or three minute induction is likely all that is necessary. Some clients who are unfamiliar with hypnosis may be a little more hesitant or resistant, and so a five to ten minute induction may be necessary. In rare cases will an induction of more than ten minutes be beneficial, unless we are trying to accomplish a specific objective in hypnotherapy. If the client has not achieved an optimum level of functioning after a ten minute induction with deepening, they probably are just too resistant; their issues need to be addressed or perhaps another session needs to be scheduled.

The induction is not really complex. It is just a script or a pattern that we use to help our client relax, feel serenity and a sense of peace. We will teach them to become aware of and control their body, and guide them to a state of total concentration.

There are six things that we want to be able to accomplish with the induction. Understand, however, that these are not all essential; in hypnosis, as with any form of communication, there are little or no absolutes, but these form a good guideline to follow.

For those without hypnotic experience, induction:

1. Guides them into a state of relaxation

2. Tests for suggestibility

3. Gives them a framework for practicing hypnosis

4. Helps a person relax

5. Focuses attention on something (example: specific imagery)

6. Detaches them from external stressors/activity

Induction guides our clients into a state of relaxation, often through therapeutic breathing. I begin most all of my inductions by asking the client to sit up in their chair, take a deep breath, and exhale. Notice I said chair. I prefer that my clients, at least initially while learning hypnosis, sit in a chair. It is possible, of course, to engage in hypnosis while lying on the floor or in a bed, but in an office setting, sitting in a chair is probably the best way to relax. A chair puts them in a position where they feel safe and in control, as opposed to lying down on a couch. Also, I do not want my client to fall asleep during hypnosis; I want them to be awake and hypnotized. A nice reclining chair is certainly acceptable, but it's still a chair, not a bed.

The second thing that we can accomplish in an induction is a further test of suggestibility. For example, we suggest to our clients that, as they *focus on a source of light or a spot on the back of their hand or something of that sort, that their eyes will become tired.* We tell them that they should *keep their eyes open until they blink. When they blink, they should close their eyes and they should keep them closed.* If our client opens their eyes after that, they are not following your suggestions.

If my client does not follow the directions exactly as I prescribe them the first time around, that is fine. I may point out that, *I see you have the ability to concentrate and focus and to remain alert; however you can also use those same energies for relaxation and to become comfortable and to let loose the muscles in your body.* We are continuing to test their suggestibility, even during the induction process, especially early on.

Third, induction gives us a framework for hypnosis. People come to a hypnotist and they expect to be hypnotized. In fact, all we are doing is utilizing natural phenomena that occurs in our client's life to help them solve problems, but that is too simplistic for some of our clients; they want to be hypnotized. So for many clients, after the pre-talk time I tell them specifically, *now we are going to do the induction. This is the part of our session where you will become hypnotized.*

I always conclude my inductions by reminding the client that *they will always hear my voice. They will continue to be comfortable and feel safe. They will accept the suggestions that I give them from this point forward.* This is a framework for suggestion that allows the client to participate in the deepener, the mental imagery that I want them to create, and to move on into the prescriptive scripts or suggestive therapy.

The fourth thing induction does is focus attention on a specific point. Most of our clients are stressed out. They are not happy, they have problems: over-eating or over-smoking or over-drinking or over-relationship difficulty-ing, etc. They come to us because life is not going the way they want it to. Their life is very stressful. In the induction process, the first five minutes of hypnosis, our client has become a very relaxed and comfortable because they are focusing their attention on something - the hypnotic process - leaving all their cares and concerns outside the door, and this is good.

Relaxation is the fifth accomplishment of induction. An induction that is particularly effective at accomplishing this state is the 'puffy cloud,' which allows them to leave their troubles floating away in an imaginary cloud.

'You are lying in a field, looking up at a clear blue sky with one white, puffy cloud floating off into the distance. Your problems are floating away with the cloud. Farther and farther away. Now 1,000 miles away." Through an exercise like this we are focusing the client's attention on something positive, and this makes them feel good. This is a positive outcome for the induction and the sixth or final thing an induction accomplishes, apart from the obvious of creating a state of increased suggestibility: detachment from the outside world, and bringing them into a state of focused attention in our office.

There are a number of different types of inductions. In fact, let me clarify: There are unlimited types of inductions, because an induction is really just a way of changing the client's state of mind. In this introductory text, however, we will be focusing on for classical inductions, including Progressive Muscle Relaxation, Eye Fixation, Visual Imagery, and Awareness inductions.

These are four inductions that I have found useful with the clients on my caseload, and I will provide a written demonstration of each here in a little while, first an overview and then we'll dissect each one. Visual Imagery, Eye Fixation, Progressive Muscle Relaxation, and Awareness approaches can be combined together, even though an induction may primarily be a muscle relaxation induction or may be primarily eye fixation induction, and so forth.

Deepeners

Following the pre-talk and the induction we go to the next step, which is deepening. The deepener is not essential but it does a couple of things for us. First, it serves the purpose of helping our clients relax further. We want our clients to enter a deep trance state if possible, one where they are totally concentrated, extremely focused, and completely comfortable. As I mentioned earlier, however, the depth of trance is not always an essential factor, so we will not always need to use a deepener. But deepeners also accomplish the stabilizing of the trance state, which is particularly important if we are using an instant or rapid induction technique. A deepener may be very brief, or you may choose one that may even take more time than the induction; it depends on the client and what it is that we are trying to accomplish.

We can use deepening techniques at any point during the session after induction. For example, if during our prescriptive script the client begins to become more awake and more alert, we can use a deepener to keep them in a heavier trance state. If you watch a stage hypnotist, after they do their induction, they usually use a short deepener and then begin their skits. If they begin to have a hard time, as in the subjects are starting to wake up or become less responsive, you'll see them engage in a skit that really serves as a deepener.

Deepeners also help to insure concentration and suggestibility. You could think of the deepener as essentially an extended induction. Often the induction is physical in orientation, and the deepening technique is more visual and experiential for our client. It facilitates imagery and prepares them for the suggestion part of the hypnotic process.

For every hypnotherapist out there, there is a different style of deepening. And, like all parts of the hypnotic process there are few limitations, but the following is an example of a very common and popular deepener, which simply involves direct suggestion and counting down: "From this point forward, you will feel comfortable and relaxed. You will hear my voice and respond to the things that I suggest and incorporate them into your life. I'm going to count backwards from five to one. As I do, with each number you are going to become more relaxed. Five...you're all relaxed. That's good. Four... going deeper now, down. Three... more relaxed...total serenity. Two...going down deeper...very good. One...all the way down now... a complete total state of relaxation."

The above is a perfect example of a simple five-count deepener; five, four, three, two, one. We are suggesting to our client that they become more relaxed with each number until they finally experience total peace and serenity, a profound state of trance. I want to emphasize that relaxation and hypnosis are not the same thing, but relaxation is a useful and pleasant gateway into hypnosis.

Another popular method of deepening that was originally applied to hypnosis by Dave Elman is Fractionation. The hypnotic principle behind Fractionation is: if a person is in a heightened state of trance and is interrupted, when they are allowed to return to the trance state, the depth of their trance will become even more powerful.

To use fractionation, the hypnotist acts like a snooze alarm, guiding the client in and out of trance: asleep - awake - talk/function - asleep - awake - talk/function - asleep.

For example:

At 6:00am the alarm clock goes off. You wake up, and feel pretty good. But you know you still can get by with a little more sleep, so you hit the snooze button and roll over for 9 more minutes.

When the alarm goes off again, you hit snooze and relax. In 9 more minutes, it goes off again. Now you are irritated; you were asleep again, so you quickly hit the snooze and go right back into sleep.

In 9 more minutes, it goes off again, this time waking you from a profound sleep and really grating on your nerves. So you hit snooze again.

When it finally goes off again in 9 more minutes, you realize you are out of time and scramble out of bed, now feeling more tired and groggy and perhaps generally much worse than you originally felt at 6:00am.

Hypnosis fractionation works in the same manner: it confuses the mind and quickly increases and decreases trance depth.

This may be somewhat be irritating to the client, but the process produces profound trance. It forces the client to concentrate on the words being spoken, and to subconsciously tune out other distractions and thoughts. Facilitating fractionation simply involves inducting trance in your subject, emerging them, inducting trance again, and emerging them, and so on, several times. Each time they enter trance they go progressively deeper.

If we combine Fractionation with the popular countdown technique, we move our client to a lower level of trance, and bring them back up to a lighter state, return them to a lower level, and bring them back up, and so forth. For example, "I'm going to count backwards from ten to one. As I count backwards from ten to one, you are going to become more and more relaxed. With each number, you'll double the relaxation. Ten... becoming more relaxed... Nine... doubling the sensation of relaxation... all of your muscles are loose. Eight... going deeper now... Seven... all the way down now. Nine... becoming more relaxed... Eight...going deeper... Seven... we're doubling the sensation of relaxation. Six... you're doing great. Eight... going deeper yet... Seven... going down further... Six... doubling the sensation of relaxation that you experience...."

This is called skipping back and forth with the numbers is a form of fractionation; instead of going directly from ten to one, we go ten, nine, eight, seven, nine, eight, seven, six, eight, seven, six, and so on. It becomes like the snooze alarm, a technique that somewhat awakens our client, makes them more alert, and then quickly takes them back down, and this is very effective at producing a profound and deep state of trance.

The staircase induction is probably one of the most popular, and it can also be used as a deepener. Basically, it combines visual imagery with a simple number countdown. "Imagine you are at the top of a heavenly flight of stairs. There are ten steps. As you step down each step, you are going to become more and more relaxed. With each step, you will go deeper into a state of relaxation, stepping out of your mind from ten to nine... from step nine down to eight..." This is a simple staircase induction, or deepener.

Pure visual imagery is also very effective. You can take your clients to a peaceful scene, such as a forest or the beach. (Remember to check that your client is comfortable with the scene you are taking them to beforehand, that they do not have a phobia of or negative associations with the mental scene you are forming in their mind).

Inductions and deepeners can always be piggybacked on each other, mirror each other, and mimic each other. Visual imagery is very effective at producing profound levels of trance, helping our clients to become deeply relaxed. One of my favorites is called the Island Deepener. My client pictures themselves sitting in the grotto of a beautiful hotel in a beautiful area where there is nothing but clear blue sea and a wonderful lagoon filled with lush green plants. In the lagoon there are five very small islands, and we will visit each one. Each island teaches them something new and creates visual imagery as they explore what is there for them to see. This is a deepening technique that brings about a feeling of pleasure, serenity, and relaxation for our clients.

Suggestive Therapy

Following the deepener is the suggestive script, for suggestive hypnotherapy. Later we will talk more in depth about specifics of structuring suggestions, how to phrase things and what to do, but for now I want to briefly touch on the methods and the approach.

We perform the pre-talk, induction, and the deepener, and then we will give our client some suggestions. As mentioned earlier, suggestions fall into two primary categories: directive suggestions and in-directive suggestions.

We want clients to respond to the direct suggestions that we give. This is sometimes referred to as skill-building hypnosis, and it is used for promoting athletic skills, for developing study habits, and for changing destructive habits.

In directive hypnosis, we are suggesting to our clients a new manner of living. For example, we might suggest that they can go to the buffet and eat smaller portions, or only eat portions that are appropriate for the specific goals they have set for themselves, or that they are no longer a smoker, or no longer fear small spaces, etcetera, and we will do this in a direct manner. "You no longer feel the urge to smoke." "You now have increased abilities to concentrate. You have the ability to draw from the knowledge that you already possess inside of you and recall that knowledge any time you choose to." We are essentially telling our clients that they actually have the capacity to do what they want and should do, by instructing their unconscious mind to align with their conscious goals, and very plainly and specifically how to achieve the success they seek.

An indirect approach is commonly used for some of the more complex difficulties clients may have, including treating psychiatric disorders. It is also a way to deal with resistance in the client relationship, because with indirect suggestion, our clients feel more like they have total control. The approach uses metaphors, and we facilitate it in a conversational fashion. For example, instead of using direct suggestion and telling the client to close their eyes, during the induction with indirect suggestion we could use the following statement: "You may choose to keep your eyes open or you may choose to close them at any time, whatever you feel most comfortable doing is just fine."

In indirect therapy, we give our clients suggestions that really come from within their own desires that we have identified during the assessment. The use of metaphors in Ericksonian hypnotherapy, which is really an indirect approach, is certainly very common, but one of the problems with this approach is that sometimes we come up with complex metaphors and our clients simply do not have the cognitive or the intellectual abilities necessary to extrapolate how the metaphor that has been given to illustrate the point we are trying to make in therapy relates to their life, so when we use metaphors in indirect hypnotherapy, we need to make sure they do not go over our client's head.

What is the best approach to hypnosis? The answer is up to the hypnotist. The best approach is the approach that works best for you, the one that you are most comfortable working with. Directive therapy is my personal inclination because it meshes well with my personality. Nathan, my co-author, tends to favor a combination of the two approaches. You should try out all styles and use what works best for you.

There are a few other components of suggestive therapy scripting that I want to talk about now. Later we will discuss writing them out and actually implementing them on a case by case basis with the clients on our caseload. And as a side note, you do not have to write out the suggestions you will be giving beforehand, but the process can be helpful to the new hypnotist. Nathan, for example, never uses pre-written scripts, as he feels the use of them limits his creativity and focus on the client. I, however, feel that scripts are a useful tool, and while I may not write out an entire script word for word, I generally jot down key words that I want to remember to include in the suggestive therapy process for each individual client. You should make up your own mind. Whether or not you eventually chose to use scripts or not, these sections the laws of script writing will certainly help you craft effective suggestions.

The prescriptive script or suggestion process is where we will use post-hypnotic suggestion, the ideas they will incorporate into their life once they leave our office. An example of a post-hypnotic suggestion in regard to weight loss is: "You will find that green, leafy vegetables are satisfying and taste good to you. When you find yourself hungry, you will choose healthy foods based on the nutrition knowledge that you already possess.' A post-hypnotic suggestion is acted upon (after the hypnotic session) in response to a trigger or specific stimulus (in this case, 'feeling hungry').

Post-hypnotic suggestions work particularly well in regards to smoking cessation. "If you ever feel the urge to smoke, you will simply take a deep breath instead and know that the craving for a cigarette will pass in three to five minutes, and in a few short days these cravings will be a thing of the past. Now relax and breathe deeply, feeling the cool clean air fill your lungs." Here the trigger of feeling a craving is used to activate the suggestion for relaxation through deep breathing. These are new patterns of behavior that our clients are going to manifest after they leave our office when the hypnotic session has concluded.

Hypnotic scripts should generally be crafted using all five senses, with a bias towards visualization, as most people are highly visual, or, on the sense most leaned on by the client (in NLP terms, their primary representational system). Suggestions should be targeted specifically for the symptom or condition the client wishes to address, and should empower the client to use their own resources in order to get over old limitations and achieve success.

Awakening

Dehypnotizing our clients is the final stage in the hypnotic process. We go from pre-talk to induction to deepener, to suggestive therapy, and then eventually to awakening our client. As I said before, it is impossible for them to stay stuck in hypnosis so we don't need to worry about dehypnotizing too much, but there are some things that are important to talk about.

Typically, the awakening is a fairly simple process, such as using the converse of our previous deepener and counting from one to five. Consider the following example: "I'm going to count from one to five. As I count up to five, with each number you are going to become more alert, more awake. You are going to feel more confident. You are going to feel energy coming through your body rejuvenating you... One... beginning to awaken. Two... becoming more alert... Three... energy is flowing through your body. You are feeling more confident. Four... almost awake.... more aware of the room around you... almost there.... Five... totally awake, totally alert."

That is a simple awakening and variations on the above theme are suitable for most clients. Awaking, however, can become more complex. Sometimes we have a client who really enjoys the feeling of hypnosis; they are in a profound state of trance, and they don't want to wake up so quickly. We may expand the awakening process for them, giving more suggestions and acknowledge the comfort that they feel. For example: "I see that you have been enjoying the feeling of hypnosis that you are now experiencing. You like this tranquil spot. As you become more alert and more energetic, know that you have the ability in your mind to choose to return to exactly this spot at any time you want to." This suggestive concept lets our client know that the good feelings they have are not a one time thing; they can return to these feelings again anytime they wish. This will typically overcome the resistance to emerging from a deep trance state.

This kind of complex awakening is generally only an individual preference, and individual needs are important. If you had all the time in the world and didn't need your office for another client, you *could* simply let the resistant client 'sleep it off' and awake naturally, but we don't really recommend that approach for the professional hypnotist.

Another approach for 'sound sleepers' is to blow a few quick puffs of air onto their eyelids. This causes an automatic response of fluttering the eyes – and they will likely pop right open – creating a more alert or conscious state of awareness.

The dehypnotizing or awakening process provides another excellent opportunity for imparting suggestions, telling our clients how to respond, how to feel, and how to interpret the session. We can give suggestions during the awakening such as: "As you become more alert and aware, you will become filled with confidence. Become more oriented to the room around you, knowing that you will now go about today feeling rested and relaxed, and feeling good and empowered to make the healthy choices."

Case Study

Now we have a very special treat for you. I have below a word for word transcript of a hypnosis session I did with Meghan, a woman who agreed to be filmed while experiencing hypnosis in order to overcome some of her own problems, and to help others learn. Even though with this written transcript from the video you miss the important nonverbal aspects of the hypnotic process, it is still an extremely valuable example of hypnosis, so study it carefully and see how much you can spot based on what we have already covered.

Richard: Meghan has agreed to participate in this short section.

Meghan: Yes.

Richard: Okay. Actually, I knew the answer to that because I referred you to a friend of mine who saw you in clinical hypnotherapy to help you deal with some issues that were important to you. Was that helpful to you?

Meghan: Yes.

Richard: Other than with my friend, Craig, have you been hypnotized on any other occasions?

Meghan: Yes. In Las Vegas at a stage show.

Richard: What happened? What was being a participant in a stage show like?

Meghan: It was fun.

Richard: It was fun?

Meghan: Yeah. It was fun.

Richard: I'm glad you enjoyed that in addition to the clinical hypnotherapy. It's easy to be hypnotized. You've been hypnotized a couple of times before. We're just going to demonstrate hypnosis. What is going to happen here is I am going to go through an induction and through some visualization exercises. I'm just going to give you some suggestions. Hopefully, it will help you feel better throughout the rest of the day, give you some energy, maybe help you increase your concentration, and enjoy the day. Does that sound like something that would be beneficial to you?

Meghan: Very good.

Richard: Okay, great. I have a couple of questions for you. Do you have a cell phone on you right now and are you chewing gum?

Meghan: Yes.

Richard: Alright, I noticed you were chewing gum. Please make sure your phone is off, and you can put the gum here. Great. Now, I want to use an induction that helps people to feel the process of hypnosis. If you would just sit up in your chair, sit up straight. You can cross your arms here for right now.

You can just begin to feel relaxed. Go ahead take a deep breath. Breathe in, and out. Breathe in, and breathe out. Deep breathing helps us to feel relaxed, and relaxation, of course, feels wonderful. I want you to feel the process of hypnosis here.

I'm going to ask you to do something. I'm going to ask you to hold your hand out here in front of you. Hold it a little higher than eye level perhaps. Just hold it out in front of you.

I see you are wearing some bracelets and bangles. I want you to hold your hand out straight and leave your hand just limp and relaxed here. I want you to find a spot that you can focus on, on the back of your hand. Maybe it's part of the bracelet or the bangle there. Maybe it's a hair on the back of your hand or a knuckle or an indentation in the skin.

Find a spot that you can focus on. Keep your eyes focused on that spot as you keep your hand rigid in the air. With your hand hopefully relaxed, focus on that spot.

It's okay to take another deep breath. Breathe in and out. As you focus on the spot, you might notice your arm begins to feel a little bit heavy. That is a normal sensation.

Arms are heavy. Just hold your arm out as straight as you are doing now with your hand limp and relaxed as you continue to stare at that spot on the back of your hand. Now, close your eyes and let them relax. Keep your eyes closed from this point forward. Picture in your mind the suggestions that I offer to you.

Your hand is extended out in front of you. I'm going to place an imaginary sand bucket; one like a child might have at the beach, over the back of your hand. It's going to hang from your hand here. It's very light. It's not heavy at all. It's a plastic sand bucket that a child might take to the beach. It, of course, comes with a little plastic shovel.

What I am going to do is take one scoop of sand. I'm going to put it in that bucket. It's not very heavy, but the added weight of the sand is something that you can feel. As you feel the added weight of the sand in the bucket hanging from your wrist, you become more relaxed.

We're going to add another scoop of sand to the bucket. As I do, you can feel the increased weight begin to draw your hand closer to your knee. The bucket is not heavy, but it is, in fact, a little bit heavier with an extra scoop of sand. I'm going to add a third scoop of sand to the bucket. As I do that, you can feel the increased weight of that sand bucket as you relax. The relaxation becomes more and more intense. The bucket becomes a little bit heavier and a little bit heavier.

I'm going to add a fourth scoop of sand to the bucket. As I do, the weight of that sand begins to pull your arm down deeper as all of the muscles in your body become relaxed. Go ahead and rest your hand on your knee. That is fine. In fact, you can even adjust yourself for comfort if you want to.

Go ahead and allow yourself to experience just a moment of tranquility and relaxation. Take a breath. Feel the air through your lungs. As you exhale, note the sensation of peace and relaxation that you experience. In your mind, you have the ability to relax at any time.

You have the ability to enter a state of hypnosis or trance. This is a state of hypnosis right now. You know that if you wanted to you could open your eyes, but you simply don't care to. Allow yourself to sink deeper into a state of relaxation.

I'm going to count from five down to one. With each number, I'd like you to double the sensation of relaxation in your experience. Allow yourself to become even more relaxed, more at peace, more rested.

Five… going deeper into relaxation. Four… all the way down. Three… let go completely. Enjoy this moment of serenity. Two… deeper yet. One… all the way down now.

Your problems are a thousand miles away. All that's left are the solutions that are inside of you. You have the ability at any time to make healthy choices and to do the things that you know in your heart are good for you. You expressed concerns about some of the difficulties that you have experienced. You have the ability to draw on the experiences you have from the past to solve the problems of the future.

From this point forward as you face the challenges of life, the resources and the strengths of friends that you have can all come together to help you become a more perfect person who is able to handle life's difficulties with pride, with power. These are things that are important to you. Those are choices that you have the ability to make at any time.

This is a state of relaxation, of peace, of total rest. When life becomes stressful at any time, you can choose in your mind to think back to this place and this time and use this experience of relaxation and tranquility to manage the stressors of everyday life. That is a perfectly good thing to do and something that you have the capacity and the willingness to do.

I'm going to count now from one up to five. As I do, you are going to become more refreshed, more energetic and more awake. You know that at any time you want to return to this place of peace and tranquility, you have the capacity to do that by simply choosing to.

There are tasks before you throughout the rest of the day. You are going to be able to complete those tasks with excitement and energy. You are going to be able to go about the rest of the day feeling better than perhaps you've felt in a long time, more rested, more refreshed than ever before.

One... you begin to feel energy coming through your body. Two... you become more alert, more awake. Three... as the energy fills your body, you begin to reorient yourself to the room around you. Four... with your eyes still closed, you feel relaxed and yet at the same time energetic and awake. Five... totally awake, wide awake, eyes open and totally refreshed.

(Richard snaps his fingers.)

Richard: That was a very brief session. How did you feel during that session?

Meghan: Relaxed.

Richard: Relaxation is good. Did you at any time wonder, am I hypnotized or am I not hypnotized?

Meghan: No.

Richard: No? Did it feel like you were doing something odd or strange?

Meghan: No.

Richard: Okay. The suggestions I gave you, how did you feel about those?

Meghan: I just concentrated on them and just relaxed.

Richard: Okay, good. Good. How do you feel now?

Meghan: Relaxed.

Richard: Do you feel good though?

Meghan: Yes.

Richard: Do you feel sleepy or do you feel awake?

Meghan: I feel awake.

Richard: Alright, great. Well, thanks for participating. I really appreciate your help today. I hope you have a wonderful day.

Meghan: Thank you.

I would like to spend a few pages talking about the above session. As I explained to Meghan, this brief session was intended for demonstration purposes, and so I hope you were able to recognize a lot the key pieces during the short experience.

We began with a pre-talk, which was unusually short because I know that Meghan knows a lot about hypnosis and she had no lingering worries to dispel. However, I did make a point to ask about gum and a cell phone (as I said, I know Meghan). During the pre-talk, we want to find out if there is anything that will keep hypnosis from being effective, or anything that may distract the client from the hypnotic process, such as chewing gum, a cell phone, things poking in their pocket and so forth, in addition to any questions or fears. I also had Meghan sit up in the chair so that she was in a more natural and healthy position. Sitting upright promotes healthy deep breathing and is actually more conducive to relaxation than slouching.

Meghan is highly suggestible, and I had actually used this approach with her once before, and so the weight of the sand bucket during induction was very heavy to her. This transcript might actually have been a little longer had I used a different induction, because I had a hard time keeping the bucket up long enough to actually demonstrate what I was trying to accomplish. This induction utilizes multiple senses and is one of my favorites because it allows people to feel the process of hypnosis in a very powerful way, which makes it a great convincer as well.

I used a basic countdown deepener because it is easy to demonstrate in this training manual, although as a rule I prefer the staircase method because it utilizes visual imagery. I generally count down from ten to one, but you can use an element of confusion and start from 30 or even 45 or even 97, and going backwards from there can be useful with some of our clients, some of the time.

The suggestive therapy process here was very simple: empowerment. I happened to know that Meghan was trying to deal with some issues in life, as we all are, and I wanted her to feel good about herself. I wanted her to know that she had the ability to draw on the tools that she already possessed to see her through, including some good friends.

I also know that Meghan has had some prior positive experiences dealing with other difficulties. I think one of the most powerful things about hypnosis is that we often draw from the experiences our client already has rather than trying to teach them new things. For example, when it comes to weight loss, my clients already know to eat well and exercise, and the difference between healthy and unhealthy food choices. I want my clients to draw from the knowledge that they already possess and use it to make empowering decisions. It is easier to have clients draw upon what they already know how to do, than to have them change to something new and different, or teach them again from scratch.

I also suggested that Meghan would feel good throughout the day. I happen to know that she was probably the first one awake in her time zone; she rises before the crack of dawn most days. When someone gets up early in the morning, sometimes by the middle of the afternoon they become a little tired and weary. I wanted Megan to feel energetic throughout the rest of the day, knowing she could complete necessary tasks with energy and excitement.

The awakening I used was quite simple. Again, this is the opposite of the deepening, so I counted from one up to five, and I snapped my fingers at the end. The snap of a finger, like a stage hypnotist might do, reorients my client to the room; it provides a sound queue matching the vocal inflection and the suggestion that I am giving, so they become dehypnotized and wake up.

This brief demonstration of a complete hypnosis session allowed you to see the five steps of the hypnotic process – pre-talk, induction, deepening, suggestive therapy and awakening – in action. Now we will work through the mechanics of hypnosis, adding more details to these steps as we go along, to build your repertoire of skills as a hypnotherapist.

At this point, however, you can hypnotize anyone. You can do exactly what I did with Meghan and people will enter a state of trance.

You now know the fundamentals of hypnosis and have discovered that it is not rocket science. Hypnotism is really a very simple thing to do, but becoming a hypnotherapist is a little more difficult. To be able to effectively impact clients and the difficulties they experience can be a demanding process, and to meet this challenge you still need more knowledge, practice and experience.

So now, let us go back and fill in the blanks and answer all the questions in regards to these five areas, and also talk about some skills that can be beneficial for creating a foundation for a healthy relationship that really meets our clients at their particular point of need.

CHAPTER 4

Key Essential Elements
for Effective Hypnotherapy

Developing a meaningful relationship with the individual client is a key to quality hypnotherapy. This avoids a ritualistic approach to hypnosis, or an approach that is not individually tailored. Remembering that each client is different, with unique needs, situations and abilities is another key. Therefore, in this section I will share with you some assessment tools that are particularly useful for creating the foundation for a beneficial hypnotist/client relationship.

Client Relationships

Strengths and Resources

The first thing we must do is assess our client's strengths. Through therapy, whether hypnosis or other forms of therapy, the sad truth is that we really don't have the ability to fix what is wrong with many of our clients. Instead, what we do have the ability to do is to take what is right and use it to compensate for the deficits that exist.

Every person on the planet possesses strengths and weakness. Chances are pretty good that the same things we don't like about ourselves today are the same things we didn't like about ourselves 10 or 20 or even 30 years ago. The things that we struggle with, the character defects, if you want to call them that, the problems that we have experienced and the things about our personality that create challenges - compulsivity, procrastination, anger - all the things that irritate us about ourselves today, are most likely the same challenges that we started with.

But I have good news for you: Even though these deficits are likely to remain in our life, we have the ability to use the strengths that we also possess to compensate for these deficits.

For example, I am the single most disorganized human on the planet. There is no one more disorganized than me. However, you cannot run a business like mine if you do not have organizational skills. So what do I do? I use my strengths: I am a good delegator and a good communicator. I hire people who are good at organization, and I use my strengths of delegation and communication to let them know my business needs, and then they go about the task of organization.

They assist me by telling me what I am supposed to be doing on a day-to-day basis. There have been times over the years when I've said, "Oh, man, this is going to be a great week. I'm going to kick back and relax since I don't have any training events to do. I think I'll wallpaper the house." Then my office manager says, "Wait a minute, you're going to Corpus Christi on Wednesday." I then stammer, "What do you mean I'm going to Corpus Christi on Wednesday? That's not until the end of the month." And she patiently replies, "No, as it's been printed on the calendar for the last three months, it's this Wednesday. And so, since this is Tuesday, your flight leaves tomorrow at four in the afternoon." Wow! I am not an organized guy, but fortunately I am able to compensate for this deficit by drawing on my strengths of delegation and communication.

We solve problems by drawing upon available resources. During the assessment process with our clients, we have to assess not only what the presenting problem is - smoking cessation, weight loss, bed wetting, depression, fears or phobias - but we also need to assess what is right about the client, what strengths and resources they possess that may be useful for achieving their goals. Later I will share with you a tool that was developed specifically to assist in identifying our client's strengths and resources.

Building Rapport and Trust

We must build rapport with our clients. Notice that even during the demonstration with Meghan, a person I already knew, I engaged in a little small talk before we began the session. Rapport is essential. If my next client arrived, and I came out to the waiting room and said, "Hi, are you... (looking at my notes) Bob? It's good to meet you. Your hypnosis session will be in Room One. Follow me. In here, have a seat. I'll be with you in just a moment, I have another client to attend to," and then I go out and attend the other client, and come back in a few minutes and say, "Bob, have you ever been hypnotized before?" Bob replies, "No, I don't know much about it. I just..." And I cut in to say, "Okay, it's a really simple procedure. I just want you to close your eyes. We're going to go into an induction now, and I'll help you quit smoking, so just do whatever I say from here on out," I have done a poor job as a hypnotherapist.

There is no rapport-building in this example, and the client is not going to trust us. For therapy to be effective, our clients must view us as someone who is on their side and fully engaged in helping them solve their problems. Rapport is essential.

Personally, I call rapport-building during the assessment process 'search talk.' Search talk is when we ask people questions about themselves. Ask any professional salesperson: if you want to impress someone and learn the keys to their (whatever you're trying to learn), don't talk about yourself and the wonderful things that you do. Instead, ask about them, what they do and like and so forth. What do you like to do for fun? Do you have any hobbies, or do you collect anything? Engaging people in small talk is search talk, asking them questions about themselves. This is a great way to build rapport and show your genuine interest in the client's current and future well being.

Trust is essential. As I said earlier, our clients are going to be sleeping with us for about 20 to 45 minutes in a typical hypnosis session, and they may not feel comfortable if they have never met us and they encounter a guy in an office by himself – especially female clients if you are a male hypnotist. The best scenario is to have a receptionist in the waiting room out front, so the client knows there are other people around. I also want to communicate trust by answering questions honestly and conveying important truths. Trust is established by being direct with clients, recognizing the limitations of hypnosis, and explaining what the experience will be like, what they should expect.

Respect and Honesty

Respecting our clients is absolutely essential. The foundation of the therapeutic relationship must be built on respect.

Early in my career as a psychotherapist, I worked with sex offenders. I was a substance abuse counselor, and the state referred people who were incarcerated to our sex offender training program. My friends and family were always asking me, "How can you work with those people?" The reality is, even though those folks had clearly not used their strengths in positive ways, and even though they had done some despicable if not downright evil things, I still had to respect them as human beings. If I did not, I could never have reached them to help facilitate change. In order to be effective with clients who are different from us – whether that means they are a different race or religion, or have different values or education, or if they are a drug user or a criminal - no matter how difficult they are or how rep-rehensible they may be to the rest of society, if they are to be our client, we need to be able to view each individual with a humanistic approach, recognizing the strengths inside that we have the capacity to draw from to begin the problem-solving process.

We also need to be honest with our clients about the limitations of hypnosis. Some clients make requests such as, "My sister was thinking about using hypnosis for breast enhancement. She is a size 34A and wants to become a 38 triple-F. Do you think hypnosis can save her $5,000 on a breast augmentation surgery?" Now, I know many therapists who would say, "Well, hypnosis is very useful in many ways. You know what the mind attends to, it acts upon. If you visualize large breasts, you will in fact eventually develop large breasts." The reality is this: I know a lot of men, who visualize large breasts every day, and they just haven't developed any breasts at all – so no, it doesn't work that way. This is, of course, a humorous example, but it does serve to illustrate that we need to be honest about the limits of hypnosis and what it is effective for and what it is not.

Do not make false or unjustifiable claims. Be honest and respect the client. Hypnosis is extremely powerful, but it is not a miracle cure for every ailment.

Openness

Let's talk about openness. I know you were not able to see this, but at a couple of points during my demonstration with Meghan – during the pre-talk and the induction - I leaned forward. I even touched her hand as I created a mental picture in her mind of the little plastic sand bucket hanging over her hand.

Openness is essential, but it is not always natural for us to have an open body posture. It is normal for us to be a little reserved especially when we meet someone new, but as a helper healer, it is important to communicate openness. In graduate school, I was taught a nifty acronym for good therapy: SOLER. It stands for: Sit down, Open body posture, Lean forward, make Eye contact, and Relax. When acted on, SOLER creates a feeling of openness, and therefore an invitation to build rapport.

Sit down; get to the same level as your client. Be open in your body posture, as opposed to radiating closed communication. Lean forward, communicate that you are with them. Eye contact is important. It allows us to see where our client's comfort level is with us, to notice whether they hold our gaze or look away, and how they respond to meeting our eyes.

Once we open up and relax, clients will 'read' this and they will relax, too. This is very important. Our goal is to help clients relax with the process of hypnotherapy. If we are not relaxed, they will pick up on this and they will not relax, either.

Equality

We have to treat our clients as our equals. This ties in with the respect issue. I like to view myself as a coach, someone who is there with my client, helping them to accomplish things, facilitating change - rather than the Superior Hypnotherapist, Richard Nongard, with Svengali-like narcissistic delusions of status, power and control. None of that does our client any good.

I tend to wear casual business attire in clinical sessions, because I believe we should strive to create a comfortable yet professional environment, not an austere business setting. Just like when they go to the dentist or to get their hair cut, clients will show up for hypnosis sessions in whatever they were wearing when they left the house, perhaps a business suit or sweats or jeans. As the hypnotist, I certainly won't wear sweats (unless perhaps I'm working specifically with sports performance clients on the field), but I will be a little more casual than an attorney or a banker, with the hopes of communicating that while I may be an expert at what I do, I'm also just an average human like they are, so we should get along just fine.

Listening

Listening is also essential, especially during the assessment process. Clients may come to us for help with one problem, but underneath are other issues. When we listen and are attentive to those things, we can pick up important cues.

During assessments for weight loss or smoking cessation, we want to listen to why the client has developed their specific habits, and what those things do for them. I believe that any time someone does something unhealthy it always meets legitimate needs, and I want to know what those needs are. For example, let's take cigarettes. On the side of a pack of cigarettes, it says, "Warning: This product may cause lung cancer." Or, "Warning: Cigarettes cause heart disease, emphysema, lung disease, and may complicate pregnancy." In foreign countries, the warnings are even more interesting than they are here in the US. In Germany, the warning label says, "Warning: This product may kill you." Canada, I think, has the best cigarette warnings. They use pictures, such as a guy in oxygen tent lying on a table in a hospital. Warning labels are direct; they tell us that cigarettes do bad things. I don't know a cigarette smoker who doesn't know that cigarettes cause problems and really can kill them.

So, if every single cigarette smoker understands that the long-term effects of cigarette smoking are death, destruction, and illness - they all know this, it is not a surprise to any of them – why do they continue to smoke? They all know that if they do not stop smoking the outcome is not going to be positive. Why do clients smoke if they know it's bad for them? Because the minute they light a cigarette, it does something for them. It helps them to relax. (At least, that's what they claim. It's really not the cigarette that helps them relax, it's the deep breathing.) Cigarette smokers have friends. At office buildings where smoking is still permitted, you'll see the smokers heading out to socialize at the smoke hole, while the non-smokers are back in their offices wishing they had a break also. Cigarette smoking gives people an excuse to have relaxing social time.

Smoking also helps people develop a sense of identity. Perceptions of what the cigarette smoker is like are communicated through media and advertising, like the cool hero puffing away in movies and magazines. Advertising works and those powerful messages are carried throughout the course of a person's life. When they light up, they instantly become someone they perceive themselves to be.

The minute someone lights a cigarette, all kinds of good things happen for them, because there is nothing bad about identity, relaxation, social networking, and taking a break. So the question becomes: Is there any other way to meet their needs for relaxation, identity, socialization and taking a break from stressors - that is considered healthy?

We need to know our client's motivation for smoking. We want to listen to our clients so that we can develop suggestive language scripts to help our clients at their particular individual point of need. We want to make sure they can still keep all the benefits of smoking, what it really gives them, without the need for the lethal crutch of cigarettes.

Availability and Consistency

The next important issue is your availability as a therapist. Now, the reality is that at two o'clock in the morning, you cannot call me even if you are suicidal; you need to be calling 911 or an emergency hot line. I'm not so narcissistic to believe that I am the only person who can help someone; I want my clients to develop situational supports outside of the therapeutic relationship, but at the same time, I want to be available. I want my clients to have my email address, but also to know that there is a time during the day that I review my client email, and I will return an email or phone call to them at that time. If they call the office and I'm not available, they need to leave a message and I will return the call when I am able. Give clients your time and ways to contact you, but also value your own privacy and promote their independence

Consistency is also important. If I see a client for multiple sessions, I want them to know not only that I expect them to be there, but I will be there also. I've heard a number of clients complain that their previous therapist kept changing appointment times on them. Scheduling an appointment during a busy work day or around children's school events can be difficult enough the first time. Don't make your clients juggle; they will find someone else to see.

Confidence

I mentioned confidence before, but I want to address it again here because it is so essential for a good client/therapist relationship. We need to feel confident about the work we do. We must have confidence in ourselves so the client will have confidence in us. Otherwise, we lose effectiveness.

Practicing is important. When I was first learning the fundamentals of clinical hypnosis, I would walk around reciting inductions, deepeners and suggestions in my head, trying to commit them to memory. I hypnotized everything in sight – door knobs (...*when I turn you to the left you will feel 100 times more relaxed...*), my pillow at night (...*three, two and ... when you reach the bottom of the staircase you will settle into pure relaxation, as if on a large, white, fluffy pillow...*), the shower head in the morning (...*when you awaken, you will feel refreshed and invigorated, ready to take on the tasks of the day...*)

because I wanted to feel confident working with clients, without having to read from a script.

Every hypnotist will have a different style and approach. Some will type out a complete script or borrow from a ready-made one they find online. Others will memorize every word and not use paper at all. Some will not memorize or read, but simply ad-lib, making it up as they watch client cues. And still others will have some parts memorized, such as the induction, but also have short notes scribbled on paper to remind them of key points to address during the suggestive therapy phase.

This last approach best fits my personal style, and as you progress with your practice and gain confidence with your skills and knowledge, you will develop your own preferred style.

I will say, however, that the more you have committed to memory – a variety of inductions, deepeners, suggestive scripts and awakeners – the easier it will be for you to adjust mid-stream to meet each individual client's particular point of need when interacting with them. Having confidence and doing the things that are necessary to develop confidence are important.

The easiest way to develop confidence is to incorporate hypnosis into your own life. Have difficulty sleeping at night? Use self-hypnosis techniques to put yourself to sleep. Are you afraid to fly? Try taking a flight on an airplane, and use the techniques of hypnosis to help you overcome your phobia or fears. Do you have a fear of snakes? I don't think you need to become a snake-handler, but you should be able to at least walk past the reptile exhibit of the zoo, and hypnosis can help you to overcome some of your own phobias. Are you depressed? You will be teaching your clients the difference between tension and relaxation, and relaxation and depression; perhaps you should learn for yourself. Otherwise, you will be far less helpful than a therapist who has got his or her own life together.

Live Healthy

Do you drink too much? Do you smoke cigarettes? Look at yourself in the mirror. Do you have a few extra pounds, perhaps because you are over 40, like me? Well, a few extra pounds are probably okay, but do you have 40, 50, 60, or 100 extra pounds? Your clients are not going to feel confident getting help from you if they notice that your life is not a model of success for them to learn from.

We can develop a tremendous amount of confidence by doing the things that we ask our clients to do, so get out there and experience some hypnosis – practice, practice, practice - and change your own life for the better while you're at it!

I would also suggest listening to some hypnosis CDs prepared by other professionals and/or undergoing a course of live hypnosis from a professional who can assist you in resolving some of the issues that you experience in your own life. I think this is important not only for you to have a similar experience as your clients, but also for you to have a clean manner of living.

This ties in a bit with the above, in that if you smoke, you should quit – unless you do not plan to see smokers for treatment (quite possibly 75% of your potential client base), or did you plan to be hypocritical? If you are overweight, you should exercise more and eat right, and so forth, for your own health, of course, but to set a good example for your clients.

Assessment and Intake

Another skill we need to develop as hypnotherapists is that of assessment. When meeting new clients and developing rapport with them, in order to present an effective pre-talk choose the correct induction method and create the proper suggestions for change, we must assess our clients' strengths and resources. It is important to find out basic information about them.

There are three tools which I personally find highly effective in the intake process – four, if you include simply communicating and asking relevant questions (search talk) – but the three tools are as follows:

Intake Form

First and foremost, you need a good intake form. You need to know your client's name, address and phone number. You need to know what name to call them by, you need their address to mail receipts or send follow-up letters, and you need their number in case one of you needs to reschedule for some reason. Personally, I also want their email address, because that is an easier way for many to communicate, including myself.

As mentioned before, we want to use our client's strengths to come up with interventions ideas. For example, if my client is quite artistic; I know I can probably be very visual with them. If they are an engineer, I probably want to be more logical or concrete. With the artist, I may use a loose, indirective visualization induction that moves from conversation right into a deepener. With the engineer or the accountant, I will probably be much more pointed and concrete.

I want to be able to relate to clients according to their individual learning style and the way that they view and see and relate to the world around them. The intake form, combined with interviewing discussion, helps give me this valuable information.

We need to discover what the client wants out of the session, making sure they have a clear and specific idea in mind of exactly what they want to accomplish, and if they have more than one goal they need to prioritize.

Understand that while there is a lot I want to know about the client, I am not going to give them 18 pages of forms to complete like at a doctor's office. The questions asked are not particularly numerous or deep, but they are relevant to hypnosis and their problems. If they had a problem when they were two years old, totally unrelated to the process here, I really don't need to know that.

I also ask them what their belief or understanding is about hypnosis, so I know what kind of pre-talk I need to give. Just because they showed up on time and are now sitting in your office does not mean they are a true believer. You would be surprised how many people make an appointment simply because they are desperate and someone said hypnosis might be able to help, but they really have no idea what hypnosis is or does – they just want their problem fixed, now.

I also want them to identify their own strengths, resources and deficits. This is a hard question at times, for anyone. What are your three biggest strengths? What are your three biggest deficits? It might sound like a job interview question, but the answers can really help the hypnotist to develop targeted suggestion strategies. We don't want to give the general suggestion of 'going to the gym a few times a week to work out' to someone who is a procrastinator or lacks time management skills. If you know up front they have a problem in this area, but have the strengths and resources of a solid social support system and extra finances, you might suggest they join a gym and set up sessions with a personal trainer. A trainer will help hold them accountable to actually make the time and show up, on time.

Ask your clients to list any medical or mental health conditions for which they are currently being treated. I want to know the diagnosis, the treating physician, and the medications. Hypnotists do not prescribe medications, and I do not think it is necessarily appropriate for us to give advice about medications to clients, however we do need to understand the impact that medications can have on our clients' lives. We could go to school to become a pharmacist, but that would take a long time and it wouldn't have a direct relationship to the work do, so the easier, faster way to become an expert on medications is to go down to the used bookstore and ask for a copy of last year's *PDR*, the *Physician's Desk Reference* for medications. It's a big fat book with every medication, every side-effect, appropriate dosages, FDA approved uses, etcetera. If my client is on a medication that I haven't heard of before, I go look it up in the PDR so I will understand what side effects there might be that could impact the client either positively or negatively.

I also want to know who their treating physician is. Depending on what I'm seeing the client for, I may ask for permission to send a note to their doctor so they can add it to their medical records that I am treating their client for whatever, using hypnotherapy. Not only is this good for the doctor to know what the patient is doing outside their office, but it is also a way to expand our referral network and meet other professionals who might refer to us in the future.

It is important to know whether or not the client drinks alcohol and if so, how much. Perhaps this comes out of my experience as a substance abuse counselor, but I know how general alcohol use can impact life. Some people who drink on a regular basis, not at an alcoholic level but frequently, have impaired sleep patterns, difficulty concentrating, focusing, weight gain and things of that sort, and they don't know that these problems could easily be caused by the alcohol they consume.

I want to know, of course, if they smoke cigarettes and how often. Maybe they came in for weight loss and they don't plan to quit smoking. I still want to know because it will affect my weight loss suggestion plans with them. Many people, especially women, do not want to stop smoking simply because they are afraid they will gain weight when they quit. You should discover if this is the case, to be more effective with your pre-talk and your therapeutic suggestions.

Do they use marijuana? Yes or no and how often. Do they use any other 'recreational' drugs? The common ones are cocaine and other stimulants, ecstasy, heroine, methadone, prescription or unprescribed pain pills and anti-anxiety medications. I want to know about their drug use history.

Now, not everyone is interested in check-marking, "Yes, I use cocaine and heroin," on a form with their name on it, so we have to assure the client that the information will remain confidential between me and them. I'm not a cop, I just want to help them. Drug use impacts brain wave functioning, and as a hypnotherapist it is important to be aware of what is going on with the client's brain.

I want to know if they have sleep difficulties. People do not function as well emotionally if they do not regularly follow natural sleep cycles. Sleep problems can be due to stress, depression, anxiety, medications, caffeine, nicotine, and a host of other reasons, and we should make an attempt to sort them out, if we can, even if they came in for a different issue, because lack of good sleep is often a Catch 22, contributing to many other problems.

I want to know about their eating patterns, because they will tell me a lot about the client's lifestyle choices, the way they abuse their body and what is important to them. I also want to know if they are satisfied or dissatisfied in their personal relationships. Depending on what brought them to my office, I probably don't need to know many specifics, a general overview will do. For other issues, however, this area will be of particular importance, especially if I am doing couple's counseling. I am licensed as a marriage family therapist, and sexual issues are a part of my domain, along with how they handle tension and stress, what they do for fun, their hobbies and so forth. And, it is especially important with couples to ask each of them, individually, what they want to accomplish with hypnosis, to make sure they are on the same page.

The last thing on the intake assessment form is the Informed Consent. We will discuss this more later as it relates to liability, but we need to let our clients know the limits of the services we offer and that they have a choice to see us or someone else at any time. We need to document that we have explained this to them and have discussed the risks (few if any) and benefits inherent in hypnosis. I then ask my clients to print their name in the space, and then sign and date indicating they understand what they wrote. Informed consent is essential.

This is the basic assessment process in a nutshell. It begins with a questionnaire and discussion about the client's particular needs, strengths, resources and deficits, and then you can begin to create targeted interventions to help the person reach their goals.

Styles of Learning

The second tool I use during the intake and assessment process is the Styles of Learning form. Each one of us has a unique learning style: some of us are more auditory in orientation, others are more visual, and others are more kinesthetic. It is important to realize, however, that while we each may have a particular style of learning best suited to us, we all learn from all three orientations. No one is only auditory and never learns or adopts information from a kinesthetic or a visual perspective, and many clients may seem to share all three styles almost equally.

These things are not inflexible. They can all work together to complement one another, and people respond to different ideas at different times. I think if we assessed someone as visual, for example, and we create nothing for them other than visual scripts, we will not serve the client well, because most people can benefit across the board from all three learning styles.

You can find a Styles of Learning question sheet on the Internet, just do a search. The one I use is adopted from work Colin Rose did on the subject, and it asks about 10 questions which can help us determine whether our client is visual, auditory or kinesthetic/ tactile in orientation.

For example, the client may make five selections under visual, two under auditory, and three under tactile. What that tells me is this particular client is oriented towards the visual style of learning, but since there are some positive answers in other boxes, all styles of learning can be beneficial for that person, with an emphasis on the visual.

Now let us discuss how these three different learning styles relate to hypnosis. There are people who learn best through sound-related experiences, they respond very well to verbal or spoken instructions. This is the kind of person you can give verbal directions to just once - "Go down Main street, turn left at the third light, head down four blocks, turn right, and when you see the fork, yield to the left, it's the seventh house on the right" - and without a map they show up at your house 20 minutes later.

Other people are more visual in orientation. They respond best to what they see and read. These people generally make better witnesses, as they tend to absorb more visual details than auditory or kinesthetic learners. They respond very well to paper maps, but if I gave them the same verbal instructions as in the previous example, they probably couldn't find the location – unless they wrote it down and/or pulled the actual address up on MapQuest or Google Maps, printed off the route, and brought it with them.

Kinesthetic learning style folks respond to the physical sensations of life, to the experiences they have with movement, textures, touch. They learn best through doing, hands-on projects and participation. They likely have great hand-eye coordination, and most often remember things by recalling what they were doing, physically, at the time.

Several years back I had a traditional therapy client who was a heavy marijuana smoker. He was depressed and wasn't doing too much with his life. His girlfriend dumped him because she didn't want to be with someone who was not motivated to do, well, much of anything. He needed to set some goals. I do goal-setting assignments with a lot of my clients; we discuss their goals and then they write them down, outlining the objectives with a pencil and paper. But I knew this particular client was primarily kinesthetic in orientation and very low on auditory, so I had him do something different.

He was about 20 years old but still living at home, and I said, "Hey, does your mom have bunch of magazines lying around the house?"

He said, "Uhhh, yeah."

I said, "I want you get some of those old magazines. Go through them, and I want you to cut out all the pictures you see that represent what you wish you had in life. For example, you said you were depressed. If you see a yellow smiley face in a Wal-Mart ad, cut it out. You mentioned that you car was a clunker. Let's say you see an ad for a brand new car you wish had. Cut that out, too. Your girlfriend just dumped you? If you see a Viagra ad with a guy and a girl holding hands walking down the beach, cut that picture out. Not the Viagra, just the happy couple holding hands part. Then, arrange and glue all the pictures you cut out on a poster board."

He did the assignment, created a poster board collage, and wow, it was really impressive – the kid had a lot of artistic talent. This is a very tactile learning exercise: cut, paste, stick, and move. It is also, obviously, very visual. I told him to take his collage and to tape it inside his bedroom door, because it's one of the first places he will look in the morning, and one of the last places he will see at the end of the day when he comes home to his room at mother's house.

Remember, this was a goal-setting assignment, so I wanted him to aim for something. I suggested that in the mornings when he looks at the pictures before heading out the door, he should recognize that those images were the things he was going to be aiming for that day.

In a hypnotic process, these three learning styles should and can easily be incorporated into the suggestions that we use. For example, when providing hypnotic suggestions to an auditory learner we may say things like, "listen to these suggestions," or, "this is what stillness sounds like."

For the kinesthetic individual, we may suggest, "Pay attention to your heart rate, feel your heart beat becoming slower and slower as you breathe in, and out. Feel the oxygen fill your lungs." These are the types things a kinesthetic learner responds to, because it puts movement, feeling and the physical nature of the body into a perspective that is easy for them to relate to and understand.

The visual learning style is easily incorporated into the hypnotic process by use of visual imagery suggestions. White puffy clouds, a staircase deepener, relaxing at the beach, a serene clearing by a mountain stream, and so forth, are particularly useful, because these clients can easily create those kinds of images in their mind.

Understanding learning styles is very important for the effectiveness of the hypnotic process. The more we understand and utilize related techniques, the better we can assist our clients with getting most out of their session with us.

Strengths and Resources

One of the most useful assessment tools that I use in my counseling practice is the NSRI: Nongard Strength and Resources Inventory. The NSRI is a simple 1-page assessment tool created by Paula Duncan Nongard to fill a real need in the assessment process. I have used it for years in my own practice, and have been licensing it to other mental health professionals since the mid 1990's. The positive feedback has been tremendous, and I think you'll easily understand the positive applications for hypnotherapy intake.

As previously mentioned, the most effective intervention ideas and suggestive scripts we can develop will come directly from the strengths and resources the client already possesses, and the NSRI is designed to help identify them. Like the Styles of Learning questionnaire, the NSRI is a self-report, meaning the client will check-mark the ideas listed that he or she relates to, and ignore those they do not.

Six sections cover different areas of life strengths, resources and abilities, from whether they have a job, to if they work well with others or alone, to their social supports and so forth. Sometimes I may know what is right about a client, but they have a hard time accepting my observations. Clients are often good at determining what is wrong with themselves, but not with seeing what is right. The items to choose from on the NSRI are simple and non-threatening, and can serve to build self-esteem once the page is covered in check-marks that they, themselves marked.

Resources are the things our clients have to help them solve their problems. For example if I were looking for a job, two resources would be a telephone and a car. So, if I am looking for a job, I have transportation and a way for a prospective employer to contact me and tell me if I am hired. Those are resources, examples of practical and useful things that exist in my life to help me solve problems.

The NSRI also measures the strengths of a person's inter-actions with others. I am a firm believer that King Solomon was right when he said, "As iron sharpens iron, so one man sharpens another." We need other people to help us solve problems. Being able to identify and integrate the client's strengths into their learning processes can be particularly useful. In order to understand more about the strengths our client possesses, we must learn as much as we can about how they relate to others.

The third issue addressed is education and skills. I want my client to recognize that the education and skills they posses are useful to them for making positive changes. I want to be able to incorporate their existing skills, qualifications and background when I am coming up with suggestive therapy programs. If a client is stressed out and feels their life has become unmanageable, it may be helpful to point out the other things they have been able to accomplish in life because they do have management and organizational skills, to show that they also posses the ability to take back control of their current situations by using those same existing skills in other areas of life.

The NSRI also surveys personal attributes. This is where we find out if our clients perceive themselves as trustworthy, helpful, friendly, courteous, kind, obedient, cheerful, thrifty, brave, clean, reverent and suchlike. I want my client to identify the character strengths they possess, because those strengths are going to help compensate for their deficits. If they want to lose weight, and consider themselves to be loyal and thoughtful, we can incorporate those traits into suggestions, such as, "... just as you are loyal to your family when they need you, you are also loyal to yourself and your own health needs, choosing to eat only quality foods with positive nutritional value that will support your weight loss goals..."

We also want to know about their situational social supports, the people they interact with. Situational supports are absolutely essential. For example, when working with smokers, it can be helpful to use what we learn here to suggest that for the first week or so of their smoke-free lives, they spend most of their time associating with supportive non-smokers, be that their mother, sister, uncle or pastor. Helping the client identify these supports up front and incorporating their names into suggestions prepares them to get help from positive sources, should they need it.

All of these issue areas can be used to help come up with suggestive therapy ideas targeted at their particular point of need. Whether you use the NSRI or a similar form, perhaps of your own creation, or whether you simply incorporate the above elements into the intake interview, what you will learn from this process will be greatly important to the success of your sessions.

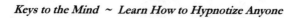

CHAPTER 5

Exploring the Hypnotic Process in Detail

Let us now return to the formal process of hypnosis, and explore the key elements of the pre-talk, induction and deepening in more detail.

The Pre-Talk

If you have never seen a stage hypnosis show, I recommend that you do so at your first opportunity, simply for the educational value (not to mention the entertainment value), as it provides an immensely powerful example of what can be accomplished with hypnosis, quite easily. Even in a noisy and often chaotic environment, stage hypnotists can hypnotize large groups of willing people - in just a few minutes.

That may sound unbelievable, but truly, as I hope you realize by now, anyone *can* be hypnotized. Unlike the eager participants in a stage show, those who are not so sure that they want to be hypnotized, and even those who might actually fear hypnosis, can still be hypnotized - *if* the hypnotist takes the time to explain the hypnotic process to them.

Detailing to the client exactly what hypnosis is, how it works, how it feels, what will happen, and how much control they will maintain or lose over what they say or do, can go a long way towards soothing the client's nerves, advancing suggestibility, and building necessary client/hypnotist trust and rapport.

Remember at the beginning of this text when I said you should have a little background information before we dove into exactly how to hypnotize someone? The information that followed was the equivalent of the pre-talk portion of this course, rather like the concepts of 'patient education' and 'informed consent' rolled into one.

With Convincers

We discussed convincers before, the tests clients can do during the pre-talk that serve to both reinforce the concepts and capabilities of hypnosis to the client, and also give the hypnotist an idea of the client's early suggestibility response level, their focused concentration level, and their ability and desire to follow directions.

I gave a couple of examples earlier, but here are a few more that you should try yourself, and may choose to integrate into your own pre-talks as you begin practicing.

The "Book/Balloon" Test

After just briefly having the client close his eyes and focus on relaxing, he is told to extend one arm straight out, palm up. He is then told to raise his other arm straight up above his head, and to make a fist with his thumb sticking up like he's hitchhiking.

Then, the hypnotist tells the client that in his open palm is a heavy book that he must support, and will simulate this by pushing down a bit on the client's open palm.

The hypnotist also tells the client that tied to his thumb is a large helium filled balloon, which is causing his arm to rise higher and higher, and the hypnotist may gently squeeze the client's thumb, for focal point emphasis.

As the hypnotist repeats and reinforces these suggested concepts over and over, more and more intensely in the next minute, the client's extended arm will begin to fall from the perceived weight of the heavy book, and their raised arm will stretch higher and higher, as if he's almost being carried away by the balloon.

When the client is suddenly told to open his eyes and finds himself in this interesting position, he is usually far more convinced of the power of hypnosis.

If, however, the client does not respond as expected, then he is perhaps either intentionally resistant, or simply unable to focus or follow directions.

The hypnotherapist should then discuss the situation with the client and determine the lack of response cause, and then overcome the problem, if possible, with further education, or perhaps simply refer the client for a different form of therapy.

Remember, for hypnosis to work, the client must be willing.

Fingers Drawn Together Test
- As if the client's fingers were magnetized.

"Hold your arms straight out in front of you, with your fingers clasped together, and then extend the pointer finger of each hand.

Now, pull both fingers apart as far as possible, and stare hard at the space between them.

You will notice that no matter how hard you try to keep your fingers apart, they are being drawn closer and closer together. The harder you try to pull, the stronger the magnet gets that pulls them together.

Focus on the space between your fingers. Try to pull harder. Can you feel the magnet? Your fingers are being drawn by the magnet, closer and closer together, until they touch."

The Eye-Lock Test
- The client's eyes close and become glued shut.

"Take a deep breath - hold it - now, as you let it out, just close your eyes and let your body relax.

Again, take a deep breath - hold it - now slowly let it out and relax even more.

Relax your eyes, and relax all the muscles around your eyes, fully and completely.

Your eyelids are relaxing and they are happy to be closed.

You are now so comfortably relaxed that your eyes want to remain closed.

No matter how hard you try to open your eyes, they will remain closed.

Take another deep breath - hold it - now let it out and relax even more.

Now that you are completely relaxed, try to open your eyes, and satisfy yourself that they remain closed."
(Pause)

"Good. Now stop trying and relax them again."

Alternative (more direct) version:

"I'm going to count down from five to one. As I do, your eyelids will lock so tightly closed that the more you try to open them, the tighter they will lock closed.

Five. Close your eyes. Your eyes are pressing down tightly.

Four. Pressing down and sealing shut.

Three. Your eyes are sealing closed, as if they were glued.

Two. They are locked shut. The more you try to open them, the tighter they lock closed.

One. Your eyes are completely locked shut.

Now, try to open your eyelids. You will find they lock tighter and tighter.

Very good. You can stop trying now. Simply relax."

The Hand Clasp Test
- Locking/gluing a client's hands together.

"Hold both hands out in front of you, palms up.

Good. Now I am going to put some glue on your palms."

(Brush your hand across both of theirs.)

"Now, press your palms together." (Demonstrate.)

"As you press harder and harder, the glue on your hands begins to set - to dry and harden - and your palms become stuck together.

The harder you press your hands together, the more stuck they become.

Press hard. Feel the glue hardening.

Your hands are now completely glued together, and even if you were to try to pull them apart, they would stay stuck together.

Your hands are stuck together. You can try to pull them apart, but they will remain glued shut.

Go ahead, try to pull them apart."

(Pause)

"Good. You can stop trying now. Your hands are no longer stuck together."

Alternative version:

"Now we're going to help you find out how strong your powers of imagination and concentration are.

Stand here, and look me directly in the eyes, and concentrate completely on the ideas behind my words.

Put your arms straight out in front of you. Good.

Clasp your palms together and interlock your fingers. Very good.

Keep looking at my eyes. Now, push your hands together as tightly as you can and concentrate on this idea: 'My hands are stuck together, my hands are stuck together.'

Very good. As you push your hands together, tighter and tighter, your arms grow stiff and rigid, stiff and rigid, as your hands lock more tightly together, as if they're made of one solid piece of steel."

(This 'stiff and rigid, solid as steel' situation is called 'catalepsy' of the arms, as will be explained shortly.)

"Keep looking at my eyes. Now, as you fully and completely concentrate on the idea that your hands are one solid piece of steel, try in vain to pull them apart, and find that they are stuck together, stiff and rigid, stuck together."

(Let them try for two or three seconds - no more).

"Good. Now stop trying, and allow your arms and hands to relax, become loose and limp, and they will release easily."

(On occasion, some people may have a little problem getting their hands apart. Just gently shake them loose and say, "It's okay, you can relax now and just let go.")

The Hot Object test
– The client holds a 'warming' object until it is too hot to hold comfortably.

"Hold your hand out, palm up. Good. Now look at me. In a minute, I'm going to put a small stone in your hand.

As the stone comes in contact with your skin, it will begin to get warmer and warmer.

As it heats up, I want you to hold on to it as long as you can, until it's just too hot for you to hold. Are you ready? Good."

(Place the stone - or other small, smooth object) in the center of their palm, and close their fingers around it.)

"The stone in your hand is now reacting and growing warmer. The heat grows gradually, second by second, it gets warmer and warmer.

The longer you hold it, the warmer it gets.

It's getting warmer and warmer, hotter and hotter.

It's like a hot potato.

It's okay to open your hand, but it will still get hotter.

Very good. Just try to hold on to it as long as you can stand the heat.

It's now hotter, and hotter."

(Keep it up until the client drops the stone, or perhaps should, due to effort limits.)

"Very good. You can put it down now, so it will cool off."

Lemon Drop Test
 - As if the client had a piece of lemon candy in their mouth.

"The mind and body work together in amazing ways. When the mind concentrates fully and completely on a specific thought, the body will automatically act as if that thought is true. Let's try an example.

Close your eyes and hold out your palm."

(Very lightly and briefly, touch the center of their palm.)

"Now, imagine there is a candy lemon drop in your hand.

Visualize the color in your mind. See the way the light glints off the sugary crystal coating.

Pretend you can feel the weight of it in your hand.

As you gently squeeze the lemon drop, listen for any sound; feel the shape and texture."

(Don't be too specific in your suggestive descriptions - the lemon drop in their mind might not look like the one in your mind.)

"In your mind's eye, notice all the lemon drop's details, as you bring it up closer to your mouth, and pop it inside...

Notice how at first the lemon drop is sweet - until the sugary coating begins to wear off - and now it's sour! Oh so sour!"

NOTE: You're looking for physical reactions - puckering face, eye scrunching, etc. They may swallow, mush their mouth around, and so forth, as they would when eating a real lemon drop.

When convincer tests are used during the awake state, they are sometimes called "waking hypnosis." At other times, variations of these tests (especially the book-and-balloon type tests) are used as deepeners during the induction process.

Muscle 'catalepsy' is a term used to describe the induced phenomena of a person's muscles locking or becoming stiff and rigid, like a board. In this state, the cataleptic limb(s) can be placed in any position you tell them, and will remain there. You can pull on a person's cataleptic arm, and it will not move. When this happens, you know for certain that the person is in a deep hypnotic trance. Stage hypnotists frequently use catalepsy tests, as it provides both certainty of trance in the subject, and also an amazing demonstration for the audience of the power of hypnosis.

Induction

With many clients I will actually say, "It is now time to begin the induction, and move through the hypnotic process from a state of alertness to a deeper level of relaxation, and trance." Any inductions that we discuss in this text, or that you learn anywhere else, are merely examples of ways to carry out the hypnotic process. Do not limit yourself to only one approach. Recognize that hypnosis is a natural process, profoundly easy to induce, and so all we are covering now are different examples of how to facilitate the process. We encourage you to learn, study, pick & chose, adapt, modify and create individual approaches that suit both you and your clients.

For more examples other than what we are discussing below you may want to look at **www.SubliminalScience.com** and download some of the free material there.

Progressive Muscle Relaxation

One of the most popular or well known clinical inductions is PMR or Progressive Muscle Relaxation. Sometimes a PMR induction can be slow, but that is okay. It can easily move a client from a level of alertness to a deep and profound level of trance. It involves, essentially, helping our clients to identify where they are carrying the stress of the day, and teaches them how to release it and relax.

As you are reading this text now, pay attention to your body. Maybe you have been sitting and reading for the last couple of hours. Maybe this is the end of the day for you because you had to work all day. Maybe it is end of the week or the end of the month. Perhaps things have been stressful for you. There is probably a spot on your body you can identify where you are carrying the tension of the day. Is it in your neck? In your back? Your shoulders? Chances are pretty good you can identify a spot.

Once we identify where we are carrying the tension of the day, we can choose to relax. We can release the tension in our brow. We can choose to relax our tense shoulders, the muscles in our neck, and back. As we make a conscious choice and effort to do this, we can feel the relaxation move across our body, and we are transported into a state of physical relaxation. As you notice your body relaxing, you may begin to realize how easy it is to also let your mind relax, and just allow yourself to open up to all the wonderful possibilities learning hypnosis brings you.

The Progressive Muscle Relaxation Induction is a very non-threatening method for first time clients. It's something people enjoy doing because everyone likes to relax and feel good. The process is simple to follow, and is familiar to many. A lot of clients who say they have never done hypnosis have listened to relaxation tapes or been to relaxation sessions, which are generally much like PMR. And I am sure you began to notice as you read the paragraph above, relaxation, both physical and mental, is very pleasant, isn't it?

"Feel the muscles in your brow and in your neck begin to relax. Loosen the muscles in your shoulders. Now feel the relaxation happening in your shoulders. Let the relaxation flow through your arms to the tips of your fingers. Feel the muscles in the chest and in the lower back... and let go of the tension in those muscles... as you relax your body feel the muscles in your buttocks begin to relax... and in your thighs and down to the bottom of your feet... and finally extending into the toes."

Progressive Muscle Relaxation generally progresses from head down to toe, enveloping the left and right sides as one on the way down. You could, of course, begin at the feet and move up, or even in the center and move out, but most people are accustomed to and more comfortable with the top-down induction technique.

A PMR induction can be performed in various lengths - short, general and directive; or long, detailed and more indirect. Which version you choose will likely depend on the client's prior hypnosis experience level; those with little or no experience or who are still a little anxious may benefit more from the longer version, while those who are eager and more suggestible should likely do fine with an abbreviated version.

Think about how you could integrate this simple yet power-fully effective approach into other aspects of hypnosis as well, such as a deepener or even as part of suggestive therapy. Also recognize that hypnosis and relaxation are two entirely and completely different things, relaxation is just a useful and pleasant pathway to hypnosis.

> ## Progressive Muscle Relaxation (PMR) Induction

- Always speak to the client slowly, in calm, soothing voice. Encouragement is beneficial, so remember to pepper your language throughout the session with positive reinforcements such as - "That's right; very good; you're doing just fine, excellent."

- Instruct the client to sit up in a comfortable position, feet flat on the floor, arms relaxed on their thighs.

- Now begin to guide the client into relaxation, by following a script such as:

"Keep your eyes focused on me. Take a deep breath, hold it, and as you let it out, feel yourself begin to relax.

Take another deep breath. All the way in, all the way out. Good. Eyes focused on me.

Again, breathe all the way in, all the way out. With every breath, let yourself relax more and more, deeper and deeper. All the way in, all the way out.

Your eyes may be getting heavy. If so, it's okay to close them now. You're never alseep, just relaxed. All the way in, all the way out."

Note: If they still have their eyes open after a few more breaths, go ahead and tell them to let their eyes close.

- It's important for the inexperienced client to know that they will always be able to hear your voice and that you are there to help them and will always be there to take care of them.

Example:

"Focus on my voice. I'm here to guide you. You will always be able to hear what I say, and my suggestions are designed to help you relax and feel more comfortable.

Take a deep breath. All the way in, all the way out. Pay attention to the sound of my voice and listen to the suggestions that I am about to give you."

- Now, have the client focus their awareness on different parts of their body, and choose to relax them.

Example:

"Become aware of the muscles in your neck and shoulders. Notice the tension there, and now choose to let your shoulders relax.

Take a deep breath and let your head grow heavy. Now exhale, and let your chin drop down to your chest.

As you become more relaxed, you become more and more comfortable. Excellent. Let your arms become loose and limp.

Take a deep breath and as you exhale, let your chest and back become even more relaxed.

Deeper and deeper, never alseep, just relaxed."

NOTE: You will suggest this type of instruction - "now focus on these muscles, feel the tension leaving, let these muscles go loose and limp" - for all areas of the body, working down from head to toe – brow, face, neck, shoulders, arms, chest, back, buttocks, thighs, calves, toes...)

- How long it should take and how detailed you need to be with each muscle group will depend on the individual client.

Watch their physical responses, and give more attention to those areas where they appear to carry more stress. For most people, 25 or 30 minutes is quite long enough; those with more experience or who are highly suggestible can easily be fully relaxed (and therefore "inducted") in 5-10 minutes.

- That's all there is to it! Now you can deepen them further and/or implement the therapeutic suggestions.

- When you are ready to bring them up, you can say something simple like:

"Now, I'm going to count from one to five, and then your eyes will open and you will feel alert, relaxed and refreshed."

As you count up to five slowly, your voice can become a little less soothing and more natural sounding with each number.

Once you reach four, if their eyes are not yet open, say, "On the next number your eyes will open and you'll feel completely alert, relaxed and refreshed. Five. Eyes open, feeling alert, relaxed and refreshed."

You may also wish to "snap" after the number five.

Eye Fixation

Another common method of hypnotic induction is Eye Fixation. Eye fixation produces a physical cue that the mind responds to; when our eyes are fatigued, we close them; this tells us to sleep.

Stage hypnotists often generate eye fatigue by having their subjects close their eyes and then point their eyeballs up as if they are looking through the top of their head. Positioning the eye this way is very tiring, and the muscle fatigue naturally causes a sleepy feeling, leading to trance.

I used eye fixation in the demonstration with Meghan by having her stare at the back of her hand or at a point on the wall. A light source can also be used, although you want to take care that it's a soft or indirect light, to protect the eye.

For example, once I was working with a client in a fairly dark room, and there was an irritating ray of sunlight coming in through the window blinds. There was no way to block the light, so I decided to incorporate it into the hypnotic process, using it as a focal point. I said the client, "What I would like you to do is stare at that light coming through the window. Just focus on the corner of the window where light is the brightest. Focus your attention on that point. Keep your eyes on that point and listen as you begin to relax." I then went on with, "Take a deep breath. Inhale, now exhale. Inhale deep, now exhale." He continued to stare at the light and I said, "Now, the next time you blink your eyes, keep your eyes closed. Simply don't open them." He stared at the spot of light for another 15 or 20 seconds and then he blinked, and I told him again to keep his eyes closed.

Adaptability is important. Instead of saying, "Darn, there is an irritating light coming into the room, maybe we should change locations for the session, or, let's move the furniture around so that we are facing the other way," we simply incorporated the light into the hypnotic process.

One of the interesting things about combining Eye Fixation with a light source is that if you stare at a light for a minute or two and then close your eyes, you may see floating clouds or trace puffs of visual imagery or photographic negative type silhouettes. Depending on the color of the light you had been looking at, you may see the opposite spectrum color when you close your eyes, purple becomes yellow, blue becomes orange, red to green, etcetera. These phenomena images can become abstract creations to draw from during the hypnotic process, as well.

Interestingly enough, a light bulb was used as the catalyst for the first ever official hypnotic induction, performed by James Braid, the man who coined the term 'hypnosis.' Braid was an ophthalmologist (eye doctor), and he would prepare clients for eye exams by having them fixate on a point of light. Once when Braid was late for a session, the client decided to save time by staring at the light as he waited. Braid walked in 40 minutes later and recognized that his client, still staring blankly into the light, was exhibiting the first signs of mesmerism. Braid instructed the client to close his eyes, and was immediately able to achieve hypnotic phenomena.

For many years after, eye fixation with a light bulb was really the only induction used. Verbal processes like those we have discussed briefly were added much later by the suggestion pioneer, Liébalt.

> **Eye Fixation**
> **- The client stares at an object or a light source.**

1. After having the client sit in a comfortable position with their feet flat on the floor and arms loose in their lap, ask them to direct their gaze at an object of fixation (a light, a spot on a wall, a specific item), and not to shift their focus.

2. Instruct the client to:

"Stare at the light (or other specific fixation object). Lock your eyes on it.

Take a few deep breaths, all the way in, all the way out. Perfect. Just keep breathing deeply.

Focus on the (object) and listen to the sound of my voice.

You will find that your eyelids may begin to get heavy, almost as if they had a heavy weight attached to them.

The longer you stare at this (object), the heavier your eyelids become, and you blink.

Your eyes feel heavy, weighted, as if something is pulling them down, as if they want to slowly close. Keep breathing deeply. You're doing just fine.

Your eyes are drowsier and sleepier and heavier, and you feel as if they are slowly closing, slowly closing; getting drowsier and more tired, and when they finally do close, how good you'll feel.

Drowsy, heavy, pulling down, down, down, slowly closing. It's getting harder and harder to see, and you feel good. Excellent.

It is very, very hard to keep them open, and you feel that very soon they will close tightly; almost tightly closing, almost tightly closing, tightly closing.

Your eyes are tightly closed; you feel good; you feel comfortable; you are relaxed all over. Just allow yourself to drift and enjoy this peaceful, comfortable, relaxed state. Wonderful.

You will find that you head feels heavier; it tends to nod forward some, and this is comfortable. Just continue to let yourself drift in an easy, calm, relaxed state."

3. That's it. Believe it or not, induction really can be this simple. Now you can deepen them further and/or implement the therapeutic suggestions.

4. As with all inductions, you can intensify this induction by carefully observing the client's reactions and timing your suggestions very closely with them.

    For example, you might make the remark, "Occasionally, your eyes are going to blink," immediately after you see the client blink. This reinforces that their behavior is acceptable, and encourages them to continue following your instructions.

Mental or Visual Imagery

We touched upon mental imagery a little bit earlier. This is another common induction technique, which can also be used for deepening. The 'images' utilized can vary from an hourglass letting out sand, to a flower sprouting, growing and blooming, to an ocean wave rolling out to sea, and countless other ideas.

However, the hypnotherapist should take reasonable care to not utilize images or objects within the visualizations that might be disturbing to the client in some way.

For example, in the following induction, the image of a 'fluffy pillow' is used. I had originally written this script to use a 'feather pillow' - but someone once mentioned that they had bad allergies to feathers, and I decided that rather than risk unnecessary resistance during the induction based on an instinctive reflex against feathers, I would simply change the object's description from 'feather' to 'fluffy,' as it would serve the same purpose.

If the client has an extreme fear of heights, using a staircase might not be such a good idea for the induction; if they are afraid of open water, an ocean wave rolling out to sea might not be so calming for them. These issues, however, could perhaps be addressed for treatment in future sessions, if the client is agreeable.

You do not necessarily need to catalog each client's allergies, fears and phobias before you begin an induction, but if your induction or prescriptive script utilizes imagery that some people are known to have difficulty with, it would not hurt to ask a general question about the subject during the assessment intake pre-talk discussion.

Another consideration for imagery induction is the client's individual learning style: Auditory, Visual or Kinesthetic. If you have used the *Styles of Learning* or other similar assessment tool, you can tailor your induction style to correspond with their dominant learning style.

The following is a more detailed example of Staircase Visual Imagery, combined with Eye Fixation and Confusion:

- **Mental Imagery**
  - The client envisions certain scenarios for relaxation.

To begin a 'visually' focused imagery induction:

- Have the client sit in a comfortable position with their feet flat on the floor and arms loose in their lap, take them quickly through a deep breathing relaxation period, until their eyes are closed.

- Instruct the client similar to the following:

"Outside distractions or sounds won't bother you; you are focused on relaxation and my voice.

Pick a point of light in the room such as a light bulb to stare at, and do not - do not close your eyes, until I tell you to.

Every fiber of your body is becoming relaxed. The day is done; problems are a thousand miles away.

Take a deep breath. All the way in, all the way out. Your shoulders, back and every muscle of your body are relaxed. Excellent.

Your find your eyelids are heavy and want to close, as if you were in a deep sleep. Soon you will be able to close them.

Let your head fall gently forward towards your chest. Close your eyes, and keep them closed.

A part of your mind knows you could open them if you wanted to, but you simply do not care to. You could fight this relaxation if you wanted to, and you know that you do not have to participate, but the smart ones always do best and are able to focus.

Easier to relax and let go. Take another deep breath, all the way in, all the way out. Never asleep; just relaxed.
Let your mind focus simply on relaxing, being reminded that a little B is just a backwards D, and an M is just a right-side E, while the 2 and the Z look the same.

Now, in your mind's eye, imagine you are in a meadow, under the clear blue sky. You see one single white puffy cloud floating high above you.

Imagine yourself lying down in the meadow, looking up. Watch the puffy cloud as it begins to float away.

The further away it gets, the smaller it gets, until it floats far, far away, and as it floats away you become even more and more relaxed.

The cloud is now far, far away in the sky, and you are twice as deep.

Now ten times as deep, and now one hundred times deeper into relaxation.

(SNAP)

Now the cloud is gone - leaving only the clear blue sky.

Even more relaxed. A thousand times deeper into relaxation.

All of your muscles feel as loose as a pile of rubber bands.

You have the ability to relax and concentrate. The smarter you are the easier it is to focus and relax. Don't try too hard, just make the decision to let go. Perfect.

In this state of relaxation, imagine yourself at the top of a heavenly flight of stairs.

There are ten stairs. At the bottom are a soft, fluffy bed and a comfortable pillow.

I am going to count down from ten, as you move down each stair.

As I say the number ten, you will relax. With each additional number, you will simply move down, deeper and deeper, one step at a time, relaxing more completely with each step, eventually resting comfortably on that fluffy pillow atop the comfortable bed.

Ten. At the top of the stairs, relaxing and letting go.

Nine. Becoming looser, limper and calmer.

Eight. Sinking into relaxation and serenity.

If I touch you or move you, this only relaxes you deeper.

Ten. Nine. Eight.

Seven. Way down. A thousand times deeper into relaxation.

Seven. Six. Five. That's fine, perfect, moving towards the fluffy bed.

Four. Three. Two. Relaxing and following my suggestions.

Five. Loosen the muscles in your shoulders and neck.

Four. Three. Two. Way down.

Three. Two. Way, way relaxed.

Three. Two. Deeper and deeper.

And finally, one. Let your body go limp. Simply sink into a more comfortable, calm and peaceful position.

Excellent. You're doing perfect...."

- Now you can deepen them further and/or implement the therapeutic suggestions.

Body Awareness

Another useful vehicle for hypnotic induction, similar to progressive relaxation, is Body Awareness. I once saw a client who came in for anxiety-related issues, restlessness, and inability to sleep. When he arrived for the appointment, he was actually shaking. Nervous by nature, he was particularly anxious about hypnosis and the process. I used an awareness induction, because it is good for those who are hesitant, resistant, skeptical, nervous or anxious. It helps them to become aware of what is going on, and to relax.

I began by pointing at a light source and he blinked a few times and closed his eyes. I then gave some deep breathing commands, which I think is one of the fastest natural ways to help our client begin relaxing. Deep breathing slows the body down, automatically relaxing us almost instantly.

I then said, "You sense yourself sitting on the chair with eyes closed; perhaps this feels strange to you being in a new place and engaging in a process called hypnosis. That's okay if it's new, if it's different, and if it's strange to you. In fact it's okay to even be a little bit nervous. Perhaps you can feel some butterflies in the stomach or even shakiness in the tips of your fingers. It's okay to focus on what your body is doing and how your body is responding. You can feel your heart beat. Perhaps at this moment, you can feel your heart beating faster than you want it to, but you have the ability to slow your heart rate down to take a deep breath in... and out... and to feel how your body responds to the experience that we are engaging in, by relaxing now."

Rapid Inductions

Formal inductions are not always necessary for hypnosis to occur. As Erickson demonstrated so well, we can simply talk to a person in a conversational manner and bring them slowly into a level of trance where they are more receptive to suggestive therapy, because they are now functioning at a lower alpha level or even into theta levels. This is especially true for our clients who are experienced and ready to get on with the process.

People ask me about fast inductions all the time because they have seen stage shows or maybe even my *Speed Trance* Instant Induction training videos produced with my friend and method originator "The Trance-Master," hypnotist John Cerbone.

A stage hypnotist invites a group of individuals up on stage and says, "Hi, welcome to the show." The hypnotist then walks up to one of the subjects and asks, "What's your name? Where are you from?" They say, "I'm Bob, from Binkelman, Nebraska." And the hypnotist says, "Sleep," and poof! Bob is out cold. Then everyone in the audience says, "Wow, how did that happen?"

Unless the hypnotist was using *Speed Trance* techniques, it probably happened simply because out of 100 people in the audience, 15 of them came forward, 10 of them were highly suggestible, and one of them already knew how to do hypnosis and was eager to be out. Those people are called natural somnambulists. They make up about 10% of the population, and they are, of course, a stage hypnotist's dream.

Do somnambulists come to our office for clinical hypnotherapy? Absolutely. They are familiar with hypnosis, they like how it feels and they know it works. You can usually say to a client who has experience with hypnosis, "We are going to enter a state of trance now. Simply close your eyes and relax. Let go, all the way down. We're in that place you want to be, and now we are going to move forward with suggestive therapy," and they are out and ready. It really can be that quick and simple.

In hypnotherapy, unlike stage presentations, however, our goal is not fast induction. There is no real benefit to a fast induction in clinical hypnosis other than saving time. The stage performer likes the process to be faster simply because he doesn't want to bore the audience with a seventeen minute induction. As a clinical hypnotist, we have already budgeted 30 or 45 minutes for the hypnotic session, so we may as well take the time and make the induction part of the learning process.

But I know you're curious, and there are a variety of methods of instant and rapid induction, many of which can take non-somnambulistic, never before hypnotized subjects into a profound state of hypnosis in less than 10 seconds. Yes, really, in a matter of seconds. However, these techniques are hard to explain in book form, as they require step-by-step physical demonstration. There are some videos up on YouTube.com of John Cerbone and I doing some of these inductions, but for a solid skills education in the art – and it is an art - I would recommend you check out the DVD set I mentioned earlier called *Speed Trance, Instant Hypnotic Inductions*, which is available at **SubliminalScience.com**.

Induction Fundamentals

– Tebbet's Six Induction Types

As you may have noticed from reading the above induction style examples, all hypnotic inductions are essentially combinations or adaptations of a few fundamental methods or techniques. These are known as Tebbet's Six Induction Types. Nathan Thomas, my co-author, breaks these types down and explains them as follows:

Eye Fixation

When you fixate your gaze upon something long enough, there is a natural tendency to begin to 'trance out.'

Fatigue of the Nervous System

Physical and mental fatigue also causes a lessening of the focus of the critical mind, and an increased tendency to accept suggestions. This is often interpreted as relaxation.

Confusion

If you confuse someone enough, they will instantly accept any suggestion that offers a way to escape this confusion. In other words, confusion causes hyper-suggestibility, or a state of trance.

Misdirection

Conscious attention is focused elsewhere, giving you a perfect opportunity to slip suggestions straight into the unconscious.

Loss of Equilibrium

When you are off balance, your state of mind tends to change, which very often lowers your ability to consciously process and reject suggestions.

Shock

Immediately after a shock there is split-second of perfect suggestibility, as their mind scrambles to make sense of what is going on. This is an ideal opportunity to slip in a short, sharp and clear suggestion, such as, "Sleep!" This, when gently and respectfully utilized, is very effective in rapid and instant hypnotic inductions.

Think about the types above, and consider in what interesting ways you can combine them when crafting hypnotic inductions. Practice and experiment with what you have learned and remember not to be bound by any limitations. Trance is a natural process and one which is incredibly easy to induce; in fact sometimes all that is required is your own hypnotic intent.

Hypnotic Intent

Hypnotic intent is having the intention within you to induce trance in your client or subject, and have them experience profound and positive transformation. When you hold this intention strongly within your mind and let it fuel your every word and action, you'll find yourself just naturally and automatically saying and doing the right things. Hypnosis will just happen, without you having to even think about it.

Practice using the techniques you have learned and then once you have experience with them and can easily recognize the effectiveness of these methods and can notice when someone is entering trance, move on from them and rely on your hypnotic intent. It might sound odd now, but have faith, it works - which you will realize as your confidence and experience grows.

Practice

It is important that you become effective at inducing trance with a wide range of people. Naturally, different people respond differently to different cues and suggestions; some people are more audio-focused, others more visual or more tactile. Some are more nervous and anxious, and others are somnambulistic. For this reason, it is important that you become proficient at determining what style of induction to use with different clients.

Through education and experience you will need to:

Develop your skills with different styles of induction.
Practice relaxation, imagery, counting and other forms of inductions, noticing the differences between the concepts/strategies they employ, and the responses they illicit.

Become skilled at noticing signs of trance.
Pay close attention to the client's physical, emotional and verbal responses to your suggestions.

SIGNS OF TRANCE:
> Catalepsy during convincer tests
> Physical stillness
> General relaxation and loosening of the muscles
> Gradual postural slumping
> "Flattening" of the facial muscles (they look very relaxed)
> Waxy skin tone (the person may begin to look more like a mannequin - this is very subtle)
> Fluttering of the eyelids
> REM type eye movements
> Increased redness or wetness of the eyes, when open
> Elevated body temperature
> Feelings of warmth, coolness or tingling sensations
> Swallowing or gulping
> Changes in breathing rate and depth
> Fingers, arms or legs twitching slightly

Positively reinforce when you see a sign of trance.
When the client responds positively to your induction suggestions, it is important to let them know that they are doing well. The client wants to please you, and hearing periodically that they are performing properly will encourage them to continue following your instructions, and help them go deeper into trance.

Adjust your suggestions to the client's responses.
When you suggest something that obviously works for the client, you can do more of it or something similar. If you try something and it does not work, quickly suggest something else of a different orientation.

Induction Accouterments

Stage performers may use accouterments or gadgets associated with hypnosis – generally made famous by movies, because traditional inductions are really rather boring to watch on film – at least in their marketing materials, such as the pendulum, fancy pen lights, metronomes, the spinning spiral or 'hypno-disc,' and so forth. Both *Trilby's* Svengali and *Dracula* made the "look into my eyes" concept of hypnotic induction so famous, and although playing the 'staring game' like kids do can certainly work as a method of eye fixation and fatigue, rarely would it ever actually be used by clinical hypnotists today.

I collect these kinds of hypno-gadgets and keep a few displayed in my office, for, I guess, thematic decoration. I don't use them with clients for induction purposes, however I have discovered that they can be great ice-breakers and rapport builders during the 'get-to-know-each-other' part of the session.

Deepeners

Following the induction are the deepeners. Again, the kind and number of deepeners are unlimited, so there is no 'right' or 'best' approach, other than whatever is best for you and your client. That said, let us explore a few of the most common types in more detail.

The Simple Countdown

I saw a Las Vegas stage hypnotist use a simple backwards countdown, and he did it, from 10 down to 1, in about 20 seconds. That's super quick, and he got really lucky that night; his induction was very strong and so the participants on stage were already in a fairly deep level of trance.

Generally, the countdown will be longer and possibly combined with other elements. For example, "I am going to count backwards from ten to one. As I do, you are going to continue to relax all of the muscles in your body... going down even deeper, letting all of your muscles become as loose and limp as rubber bands. Ten... making sure that the muscles in the brow are relaxed... 9 ... letting loose the muscles in the neck and shoulders... 8 ... continuing to relax the arms and the fingers... 7 ... relaxing the torso and your back... 6 ... feeling the relaxation through your legs and through your knees and through your thighs... 5 ... becoming even more relaxed ..." and so forth.

The above is an example of a ten-to-one simple countdown combined with Progressive Muscle Relaxation reinforcement. You do not have to combine with anything, simply counting down is fine too.

It all works - if we are confident with the client, if our client wants to be hypnotized, and if we have done a good pre-talk.

The Dave Elman Induction/Deepening Technique

You can use this technique as either the induction or the deepener; they are interchangeable. And, when you think about it, in many ways the induction and the deepening are very similar, aren't they?

This technique asks for the occurrence of client-generated hypnotic amnesia as a phenomenon. The client does most of the work themselves, and perhaps this is why it is so effective.

You will instruct the client to begin counting down out loud from 100 or from 50 or wherever you want to start. As they say each number aloud, they are to visualize the number fading away, until eventually, usually by the third or fourth count; they cannot see nor remember which number comes next. As this occurs, they will find themselves going deeper and deeper into trance. Often the hypnotist will instruct the client to say, "deeper and deeper" or "deeper and more relaxed" between each number, because this is a self-suggestion which makes the deepening occur even more quickly.

For example:

"I am going to ask you to count backwards, out loud, from fifty to one. In your mind, I want you to visualize each number as you say it out loud. And then, I want you to say, "Deeper and deeper," and as you do, the number will just fade away into nothingness. After a few numbers, they will all be gone quickly, leaving nothing but relaxation behind.

"Begin now. Fifty... deeper and deeper. And the 50 fades away. Very good. Forty-nine... deeper and deeper and it fades away. Excellent. Notice that as you count, you have trouble with which number follows next. It is okay to forget the numbers as they fade away and you relax deeper and deeper. Forty-eight... deeper and deeper ... and the numbers fade away. The relaxation doubles and you feel good... Just let the numbers disappear now. You can let them fade away to nothing; relaxing deeper and deeper...until all the numbers are gone and you are so relaxed. Are they all gone?"

Staircase Deepener – Mountain Path Variation

The staircase deepener, like the number count, is a concept that can be molded and adapted a million different ways. Personally, when I use a descending staircase countdown, I generally have the client create in their mind a relaxing, fluffy bed with a big fluffy pillow waiting for them at the bottom of the stairwell, which helps them to step down in their minds into a state of total rest, relaxation and serenity.

A similar deepener which utilizes visual imagery and implied fatigue is the mountain deepener, which may go something like this:

"I want you to picture in your mind that you are in the rolling foothills of a mountain range. It's a beautiful day. The hills that you are traveling are not very steep. You notice a path between the hills that is easy for you to follow. In your mind's eye, begin walking down that path through the rolling hills. As you do, you'll find that it's serene and peaceful, a relaxing experience for you.

As you move through the hills, you notice the path becomes a little steeper. As it becomes a little steeper you have to use a little more energy to go up the path. As you do, you feel relaxed. You are enjoying your surroundings... the birds in the air above, the fresh air that you are breathing.

As you continue along the path, you find that it becomes a little more difficult to travel... You find it little more difficult because it's becoming a little steeper still. The path from the hills leads to the edge of the mountain, and you find a place where you can comfortably relax. It's okay to rest for a few minutes on this path...

As you journey on the path up to the mountain, you find that it brings you an overwhelming sense of peace. The path becomes perhaps a little narrower in some spots. That's okay though because you have found a walking stick. The walking stick can guide you through the parts of the path that are a little steeper and little more difficult.

As you continue along you'll find that you are even higher. You can look around and see the other mountains in the distance.

They look so close. It seems like you could almost touch them. In your mind, you know that they are actually miles away. This plateau is a wonderful resting spot, but we are going to continue on the journey up this narrow path, up this steeper hill, to a spot where we focus on resolving some of the issues that you have presented today."

With this mountain deepener, we are taking the client through a peaceful and relaxing experience which can also act as a hypnotic metaphor for the process of problem-solving. For example, in the following suggestive therapy phase, I would perhaps say to the client:

"Like our journey up the mountain, losing weight sometimes has difficult places along the way. Some roads are rocky or narrow. You might not feel like you have all the choices you want to, but you know that within you, you can make the choices that are necessary for healthy eating and progress. Like the walking stick that guided you through those steep and narrow paths up the mountain, the knowledge that you have about healthy foods and nutrition choices can be a walking stick to help you make decisions that are good for you. Your friends, your family, the supports that you have will all be beneficial to you as you journey along the path of being successful at achieving your weight loss goals."

When using deepeners that incorporate imaginative journeys of visual imagery, I encourage you to be creative. Think of scenes that your clients will relate to and enjoy, and whenever possible incorporate all five senses into your hypnotic description. You can also be ambiguous enough to allow your clients to create the scene themselves, for example, 'allow your imagination to take you to a certain place where you feel comfortable and safe...'"

You can even talk to your clients during the hypnotic state and have them describe and explain to you what they are experiencing, and use this to give them an empowering hypnotic journey which acts both as a deepener and a therapeutic metaphor based on exactly what their own preferences and needs are.

Practice talking to your clients and experimenting with hypnotic journeys and imagination exercises, and experiment with new ideas – remembering, of course, to make sure that the client is okay with the kind of scene you are creating.

Fractionation Deepening

Remember the annoying snooze alarm we discussed that sends you deeper every time it goes off? Another fractionation technique has a client close her eyes, and then she is asked to open her eyes, and then asked to close her eyes again, and again. This is known as Vogt's Fractionation, developed by German hypnotist Oskar Vogt in the late 19th Century.

Vogt's fractionation or a variation thereof, is how stage hypnotists keep a show going. It is easy to bring someone up to light levels of the trance, have them respond to suggestions, and then instantly take them back down into a deeper level of trance. At a stage show, the hypnotist performs the induction, and then the deepener, and then the first skit. A lot of times the first skit has the subjects playing an imagined musical instrument, or perhaps a hot and cold skit where they experience minor kinesthetic hallucinations as their body temperature changes.

These are called deepening skits, and they familiarize the subjects with the hypnotic process. In stage hypnosis, suggestions move from the easiest things to do, to the most difficult, and between each skit the participants are awakened - eyes open, wide awake - and then put back to 'sleep' by the hypnotist.

Asking them to wake up, do things, demonstrate hypnotic phenomena and go back to sleep is a fractionation technique. After this happens many times throughout the show, the subjects are in a very deep level of trance and are ready to perform more challenging demonstrations such as hypnotic amnesia and muscular catalepsy.

In a clinical setting, Vogt's fractionation is used in less entertaining ways, but for the same purpose of deepening the trance state. A session utilizing Vogt's fractionation will be fairly long because one, it can take a little while with the awake/asleep/awake/asleep process, and two, you will want to maximize the suggestive therapy use of the profound state you have spent time creating.

The following is an example of what one could say when using fractionation combined with visual imagery primarily as a learning process, getting the client accustomed to hypnosis and figuring out how best they respond.

(And just so you understand, for demonstration purposes in this text I am going through this far more rapidly than I would with a client. Rarely, in a clinical setting, would we do such rapid visualizations or Progressive Muscle Relaxation exercises. You will need to use your own intuition and common sense to add pauses and details. You will also need to incorporate client-targeted positive suggestions and other sensory experiences.)

"What I would like for you to do is close your eyes. I would like you to imagine that you are sitting in a field on a beautiful spring afternoon. The weather is just perfect. You can feel the sun on your skin, but you are not too hot and you are not too cold.

As you look at sky, you see that it's a clear blue sky. In that clear blue sky, you see one single, white, puffy cloud. As it gently and lazily floats through the sky, it begins to disappear into the horizon.

As it becomes smaller and smaller, as you look at that cloud, you become more and more relaxed... As the cloud becomes tiny in size, you realize it has disappeared into the distance...

I am going to count backwards from one to three, and as I count from one to three, you'll become more awake.

You will reorient yourself to the room and you'll open your eyes. One, two, three... (Snap)."

Now our client is in a normal state, and you may want to ask them, "Were you able to see the pictures in your mind? Did you see the puffy cloud? Was it moving slowly? What were the images like? Could you actually feel the sun on your skin?" We ask about their experience because that will let us know for sure that are they visualizing. If they are not, perhaps we should be focusing on another representational modality, such as kinesthetic or auditory suggestions.

Now, we would ask the client to re-close his/her eyes, and run them through a quick progressive relaxation re-induction to see how they respond, and then emerge them (1, 2, 3, wide awake) once again, and ask about those experiences.

At this point we have learned about the client's responses to imagery and relaxation. Perhaps now we'll do an eye-fixation re-induction with a number countdown. And again, we would wake the client and ask them about their experiences, and then we would possibly go on to say:

"You are really getting the hang of this. Doing a good job. I am going to spend a couple of more minutes with you, and during that time, I'm going to again help you to achieve a level of hypnosis to relax both your mind and body, and help you make some changes in your life."

Then we will do another re-induction and deepener, and then finally get on with the therapeutic suggestion phase. Although the description above is brief, this outline represents Vogt's fractionation at its finest.

There are many other ways of utilizing fractionation deepening, such as with rapid inductions. You would do a rapid induction, followed by a quick awakening, then a rapid re-induction, again and again, so that 4 or 5 phases of fractionation (awake/asleep) fit into about a minute. This can be quite effective when you have the confidence to pull it off.

This approach may also use post-hypnotic suggestions as a trigger for re-induction, especially if you use suggestion to augment the natural effect of fractionation. For example, after the first induction you could say, "I am now going to count from 1 to 3, and when I reach 3 you will be wide awake and fully alert. However when I say, '3-2-1-sleep,' your eyes will close, your head will drop, and you will immediately return to a deep and comfortable state of trance, going at least ten times deeper every time we do this.'

This technique not only enhances the effect of the fractionation, but it also begins to build credibility with the client, as they will, of course, respond perfectly to this suggestion.

Since there are unlimited ways of inducing hypnosis, there are also unlimited ways of deepening the trance state, so experiment with the approaches that suit you best, to develop your own style and approach. Let the words flow from your mind and ensure you always speak from a state of comfort and relaxation. Describe to your clients what it is like to be in trance, and they will follow you there.

CHAPTER 6

The Art of Suggestion
~ The Heart of Hypnotherapy

Suggestion is viewed as the heart of hypnotherapy, and is something that many traditional psychotherapists are not familiar with. In counseling programs, we were taught Rogerian techniques to reflect back what we thought we heard our client say. This approach does not answer questions nor give advice, but puts it back on the client.

For example, if a client says, "Richard, I have a question for you. I have a choice to make between these two options. Which one should I choose?" As a traditional therapist, I would likely simply reflect back what I thought I heard the client say: "Well, Mr. Client, what I think I heard you say was that you wondered what choice I would make out of two options...."

To me, a Rogerian approach in therapy is somewhat like an Ericksonian approach in hypnosis, believing that our clients have within them everything they need already, and that they will have an 'ah-ha' experience and generate their own insight when questioned. It has been my experience, however, that most of my clients in therapy don't ever generate that 'ah-ha' experience. Directed therapy and directed hypnotherapy that actually gives suggestions can be beneficial to our clients, but this approach is often resisted in traditional therapy.

Suggestion is powerful and effective. For those who are uncomfortable with suggestion (basically, telling someone what to do) because of your background or personality, let me tell explain a couple of things. First, our hypnosis clients expect suggestion. They come to a hypnotist to make positive life changes through the process of hypnosis, and that process involves the subconscious mind receiving positive suggestions, and this is what they expect. Secondly, our clients like hypnotic suggestions because it makes life better and easier for them. If they could achieve the same things on their own, they would have done it. Hypnosis helps, and they like that.

Suggestion in general, even without hypnosis, is highly effective. If it weren't, there wouldn't be so many advertisements everywhere. Every image in a magazine, slogan on a poster and jingle on the radio is a suggestion for you to do or buy something.

It really is amazing how responsive people are to sensory suggestions. The next time you're sitting around the lunch table with a group of people, grab a fresh carton of milk. Open it up, take a sip and just say, "Oh, gosh! This milk is putrid, horribly rotten! Here, smell that." Then, pass the carton of good milk around and watch what happens. Because you gave the suggestion that the milk was bad with conviction and confidence, they will respond physically in a negative way, and everyone who smells the carton will respond to the putrid, nasty, awful milk – even though the milk is perfectly good.

Have you ever yawned just because you saw someone else yawn? This is yet another example of why suggestion is a very powerful and prolific change agent, and can be used to great effect in the therapeutic process. Are you yawning now?

Because suggestion is so powerful, we need to recognize that it can be misused. Most of the clients on our caseload would never act on a suggestion that was contrary to their own moral beliefs, but some clients are more suggestible than others, and could be abused by an unethical hypnotherapist. Every now and then there are cases of unethical psychiatrists, social workers and counselors abusing their clients. And, every now and then there are also stories of unethical hypnotherapists who take advantage of their client's suggestibility.

Consequently, this is one of the main reasons why people fear hypnosis. When it comes to civil litigation lawsuits in psychotherapy, probably the three biggest psychotherapeutic errors that clinicians make are: failure to recognize the power of therapeutic relationship, failure to recognize the limitations of their training and technique, and failing to respect the client. The same errors apply to hypnotherapy.

It is a very contentious and hotly debated issue among hypnotists as to whether someone can be hypnotized to do something against their own will. Many hypnotists maintain that you cannot, while others claim that morals and wills are only surface veneers, which themselves can be changed by skilled and unethical hypnotists. Whatever your own beliefs on this matter are, it is crucial that you always recognize the power of suggestion, and respect your client.

Principles of Suggestion

Let us now take a closer look at some principles of suggestion. These are guidelines, not hard and fast rules, but they are helpful to bear in mind as you craft hypnotic suggestions.

Be Positive

First, suggestions should be phrased in the positive. We want to say, "You enjoy breathing fresh breathing air," rather than, "Whenever you smoke, you will become sick by the noxious air that you are breathing in, and you'll cough uncontrollably." There is a difference in results. Instead of helping our client to stop doing something, I want them start doing something positive. Instead of suggesting, "You will quit biting your nails," suggest the positive, "You will enjoy seeing your nails grow long and even." That is not to say you can never phrase suggestions in the negative, or never use 'don't' or 'stop' language, but as a rule, tell them what to do, rather than what not to do.

Be Clear

Suggestions also need to be understood by our client. Our metaphors and suggestions need to be constructed appropriately for the individual client's age and level of cognitive and moral development, so that they don't go over the client's head. In general, suggestions that they can instantly understand on a practical, functional level are better than complex suggestions for which they need to use their conscious minds to decipher.

Stay Focused

Suggestions should focus on single topic, rather than multiple ideas. As with cognitive-behavioral therapy, the suggestions given will focus on specific identified issues, problems or situations, and are designed to provide alternative relief strategies or goals. The "you will quit smoking, lose weight, and start being nice and cleaning house every day" all in one round approach is simply not effective. Some suggestions and improvements do go hand in hand, such as confidence and self esteem, however, as a rule, focus on providing change-suggestions for only one major issue per session, so that you can help the client to fully focus on it.

Stay In the Now

Suggestions should also be in the present tense, rather than the future or past tense. People come to you because they want to change, and so you might as well help them make those changes now. Instead of suggesting, 'In 3 to 6 weeks you will be a non-smoker," suggest, "You are now a non-smoker, a happy, healthy and smoke-free individual."

To support present-tense suggestions, we may use post-hypnotic suggestions. Post-hypnotic suggestions are new patterns of behavior given during hypnosis, with the intention of being incorporated into the client's life following hypnosis. These directive suggestions give the client an answer down the road outside your office for what to do when faced with a challenge. For example, "You are continuing to lose weight and feel great. If you feel the urge to snack, you will reach for healthy, natural foods, instead of processed chips and dip or cookies."

Be Educational

Hypnosis is a learning tool, and hypnotherapy often makes use of metaphors during suggestions in effort to show how specific concepts, perceptions, actions, beliefs and goals may relate, as well as to convey concepts which can later be translated and applied to multiple situations. They are also frequently used as relief mechanisms, particularly for clients needing stress management help.

For example, "Your daily stress is like the leaves of a tree. It builds from the roots, and then rises. See your stress rising up through the trunk, and travelling out along the branches, thinning and thinning as it flows upward and outward, getting smaller and smaller as it reaches the end of the thin branches, then even smaller as it turns into beautiful green leaves. See the green leaves turn golden, then brown, and now watch them detach, fall off and float to the ground, discarded and no longer necessary, no longer existing."

Remember, however, that whatever the functioning level of the client is when they are awake, will be the functioning level of the client when they are asleep. You must tailor the therapeutic language of your prescriptive scripts – including metaphors - to meet the intellectual, educational, social, economic, physical and emotional functioning levels of the individual client. If they would not be able to grasp the metaphorical relationship between 'the view of a sunrise from atop a mountain' and a 'positive outlook on their future marital relationship' while awake, they will not be able to do it under hypnosis.

Be Realistic

As we discussed earlier, suggestions should be based on the client's strengths, and should be attainable. Someone seeing you for weight loss is not going to lose 40 pounds in one week, so do not make unrealistic suggestions. Suggest progress, constant realistic and impressive improvement, such as, "You will continue to lose weight at a rapid and healthy pace, to the point where you are at the ideal weight for optimum health. You will be surprised by how fast you lose weight when you increase your exercise and make healthy food choices, and you will feel great noticing yourself become slimmer and healthier as time goes by.'

Utilize the Senses

I think suggestive therapy should also incorporate the five senses. Visual imagery (what the client sees), olfactory descriptions (what the client smells), tactile descriptions (what the client feels physically), sound (what the client hears), and taste, during the practice of the suggestions are all important areas to address. The more senses you can work into the suggestions used throughout the session, the greater the efficacy will be.

For example, "You are beginning to see yourself as a more confident individual. You can really feel this growing confidence surging through you. The idea that you are confident just sounds right, and when you realize just how confident you really are, you will truly be able to taste the victory you have earned.'

Remember as well that most people have a dominate visual learning style, and so visual suggestions can be highly effective. The client may be instructed to visualize the desired goal or outcome as if it were already achieved to perfection, and/or to visualize themselves working through the identified problem and reaching the desired conclusion.

For example, they may see themselves relaxed and reading a book on an airplane (instead of anxiously fidgeting), or speaking confidently in front of a large group (instead of sweating and stuttering). As you can see, there are many other ways of incorporating multi-sensory descriptions into the suggestion process, so take care to give rich and meaningful suggestions.

Additionally, hypnotherapy is quite effective for treating numerous physical problems and symptoms, and therefore sensory suggestions related to body awareness are commonly used for those who are nervous or have anxiety disorders, as well as those who lose focus due to body preoccupations. Suggestions may be given to control breathing or heart rate during stressful situations, to raise or lower body temperature for sports activities, and even to minimize or eliminate allergic reactions.

Body awareness suggestions are also frequently used for pain management - becoming aware of the absence of pain. For example, "You can feel the hurt leaving the pain. There is less intensity now."

Suggestions should also relate directly to the individual client's goals and presenting problems, rather than come only from a prepackaged, inflexible script.

Therapeutic Suggestive Scripting

The world of hypnotherapy is full of scripts - scripts you have written, scripts others have written, scripts that you can download from the internet or purchase in books. There are prepackaged scripts available on just about every subject you can imagine.

These scripts are useful; they can provide direction or guidelines for addressing specific issues, and most of the time, the author has taken the time to use specific language and phrasing deemed beneficial or effective. However, as mentioned before, every client is different, and has not only different strengths and resources, but also different needs.

Not every client needs to lose fifty pounds; some only wish to drop a few pounds and tone up their muscles. These are different goals, and will require a different strategy when creating suggestions.

Especially when you are less experienced, it is fine to use these scripts as a tool for both understanding the hypnotherapeutic process and implementing suggestions - but you also want to take the time to tailor the script to meet the specific needs of each individual client.

The scripts are not written in stone, and can be easily modified; you may substitute individual words (fluffy for feather) or entire concepts (climbing stairs instead of a mountain). You may take a section from one script and insert it in another.

As you become more experienced, you will likely rely less and less on complete scripts, and instead you may utilize a hastily sketched outline that you develop during the intake/assessment process, designed to meet the specific needs of the client.

And remember the Law of Dominant Effect: A stronger emotion will always replace a weaker emotion. Attach significant emotions to change when forming suggestions.

The mind is an amazing machine; modern computers can hardly rival its ability to categorize and index thoughts, feelings, sensations, corollary relationships, entire experiences, and so forth. Each item in the mind's database is simultaneously organized chronologically, by intensity, by location, by time, by person, by emotion, by smell, by preference, by pain, and so on.

When you suggest that the mind retrieve an emotion, the mind will assess its meaning, function, relevance, relationship, and intensity to everything in its database. To facilitate positive change, the hypnotherapist needs to get the mind's attention in a big way. Using suggestions with stronger emotional impact will increase efficacy for change.

For example, "Now that you are a nonsmoker, you are enthusiastic about life, and feel as energetic as a person ten years younger," is far more attention-getting to the mind than, "When you quit smoking, you will feel better."

Better, relative to what? Better is a generic term that the mind will pass over as being less important and intense than even 'good' -- and "when" is not concrete or specific.

Better than you felt yesterday? That is more specific, but still not dramatic enough to take much notice. Better than ever before? Well, that is better, but is still neither specific nor intense enough to cause the mind to take active interest.

Good -> Better -> Decent -> Great -> Wonderful
-> Fantastic -> Amazing

Give the client's mind specific emotional cues, using terms associated with high intensity.

These are some thoughts in regards to suggestion that I hope you are able to incorporate in your hypnotherapy practice. It can be a lot to take in one go, so practice, practice, practice and soon you'll just find yourself naturally incorporating these principles into the hypnosis you do without having to really think about it.

CHAPTER 7

Abreaction, Practice and Referrals

Although hypnosis is nearly always a safe and pleasant process, occasionally things can be disturbing or go wrong, and your subjects can abreact. While this is uncommon it is also very important to understand, and so I felt this subject deserved a chapter to itself.

We can define abreaction in a number of ways. In the broadest sense, since hypnosis is generally regarded as a relaxing experience that makes one feel good, abreaction then can be defined simply as a "bad trip' or unpleasant experience in hypnosis. Although abreactions are extremely rare, it is crucial that you learn how to handle them confidently and professionally.

An abreaction is a state of intense emotion, where a person is actually re-living an experience that perhaps traumatized them in the past. It is not simply a state where they are a removed, casual observer of the bad things they have experienced (like during the Fast Phobia Cure - you can find information about this technique online), but where they are experiencing all over again the trauma, the misery and the horror of past suffering, as if they were actually right there in person at that moment and time.

Abreactions can occur spontaneously, and they can be created or induced by the hypnotist - either deliberately as part of a therapeutic process, or accidentally when the hypnotist acts unsafely. Typically, abreactions occur during age-regression phenomena or therapy, which is a hypnotic process or method that requires a lot of training and experience to pull off safely and effectively.

When used properly, a therapeutic abreaction has only two purposes: First, to discover what happened, and second, to discover who, if any, the players are. Once this information is determined, the hypnotherapist should terminate the abreaction and begin transformational therapy.

At this stage in your training, please, please, please do not attempt age-regressions!

Abreaction can also be spontaneous. For example, imagine a client was suggested to regress back to a time when they were eight years old. Now, a stage hypnotist giving this kind of suggestion would likely intend for the subjects to act child-like and be goofy silly, like little kids are. However, what if one of the participants had a fire at their house when they were eight years old and a sibling died. They were terrified and scarred at least mentally if not physically. An abreaction would cause the subject, now feeling eight years old again, to re-experience the heat of the flames, the terror of the emotions, hearing the cries of the brother who was lost in the fire, and so forth. Not a pleasant thing to re-experience, and definitely a stage show killer.

When some clinical clients are hypnotized, they will suddenly fall into abreaction and start crying, yelling or flailing about, because they have regressed to a traumatic event on their own. We could be doing a session and suddenly a metaphor brings our client spontaneously back to an emotionally or physically traumatic situation. For example, perhaps we used the mountain climbing metaphor from earlier, and perhaps the client was once trapped on a mountain or caught in a flash storm or even just broke an ankle on a trail. We will be able to see the trauma on their face, in their physical responses, and possibly in the language they use as they abreact.

Unfortunately, you cannot pre-determine which clients might do this by looking at them or talking to them. The subconscious mind sometimes protects a person from having to deal with traumatic events - such as rape or a terrible accident - by blocking that event from their conscious memory; so while they may appear to be emotionally well-adjusted on the outside, they are actually subconsciously suffering from some deep emotional situation, which may spontaneously resurface under hypnosis.

Again, spontaneous abreaction is not common, but it can occur at any time and we should be ready for it. We will discuss what to do about it in a few minutes.

As mentioned earlier, abreaction can also be intentionally induced. Some hypnotists, and regular therapists too, will deliberately cause abreactions as part of therapy, believing that being able to re-experience the fears, traumas, difficulties or hardships in our life can teach us lessons we need in the present, to resolve and come to terms with those difficulties. Personally, I think that directed abreaction is probably overused, but that it does have therapeutic value particularly with post-traumatic stress disorder.

The intrusive mental images or pictures, olfactory sensations, sleep disturbances and all the signs and symptoms of PTSD that occur following a traumatic event are caused by the victim's mind trying to make sense out of what happened. Re-living traumatic events is a natural process we all go through in order to come to terms with them and understand what they mean.

For example, I was in a serious car accident when my son was six months old. I was driving down the road and this guy was turning left out of a parking lot. He apparently looked left, then right, but failed to look left again, hit the gas, and smashed into the passenger side of my car. It was a horrific accident. Car seats then weren't what they are now, and my son was flipped all around and ended up upside down, not breathing and bleeding out of his mouth. All I could think was that in movies, that's what dead people do. I bailed out of the driver's seat, wrenched open the rear door, and grabbed my son up, car seat and all. I didn't wait for the ambulance to show up; we were near a hospital and I flagged down the first car I saw and screamed, "Take me to the emergency room!"

I was in shock, and I remember yelling at the driver to drive faster and that I had a dying baby. It was very traumatic and difficult for me. The emergency room had been called ahead. I have no idea who made the call but they were waiting when the dear, sweet lady dropped me off. The doctors took my son from me and ran into the building. Then, there I sat waiting for about five hours. I'm sure you can imagine how I must have been feeling during that impossibly long wait. Finally, I was able to see my son in the pediatric intensive care unit, and miraculously he eventually made a full recovery.

One of the things we know about memory is that people don't have memories before the age of 24 months that stay with them throughout life, so although physically my son suffered much more, it was I who experienced the psychological trauma.

Later in the day, the police officer who was investigating the accident came to talk to me at the hospital. He has a little clipboard and he's asking me questions. He says, "Okay, Richard, when was the first time that you became aware of the truck?" To which I replied, "Look, I've got stuff to do. I mean, I'm not feeling so good. My ribs are cracked; my son is up in intensive care, so ask me questions later. It was the other guy's fault. I've got to go." But he was persistent. "I just need to ask you a couple of questions. I want to know about the truck." At this point I'm so on edge it's all I can do to remain remotely diplomatic. I said, "There was no truck. A freaking Chevy Corsica drove into me, some dude in a blue Corsica. You must have me confused with some other accident if you're asking about a truck." I started to walk away and the officer grabbed my shoulder, stopped me, turned me around and said, "Yeah, a blue Corsica hit you. But that's when you crossed over towards the oncoming traffic and hit the semi truck."

He wanted to know when I first became aware of the truck, and the answer was right then, when he told me about it, six hours or so after the accident occurred. I had been in such an emotional state and so focused on the crisis at hand in regards to my son that I was totally and completely unaware we had hit a semi truck across the road.

The next several days were a blur. About week later, I had to drive to Fort Worth, Texas to do a training session. I remember driving down the open interstate, no traffic, not a car within miles, and I'm physically responding to imaginary trucks driving into my car. My mind was trying to make sense of it all – with what I knew had occurred a week earlier, and what I had been told happened.

I relived the accident in my mind thousands of times over the next month. It is a natural process for our minds to want to make sense out of what has happened to us, to consider how it might have turned out differently, either way. "If we had been hit by the car one more inch forward, we would have been dead," or "If I had only swerved it wouldn't have happened at all," and so forth.

Personally, I re-lived both what I knew (how we were hit by the car), and tried to sort out the part I didn't know (where, when, why and how we hit the truck). These were intrusive mental images that really distressed me for a period of weeks following the accident. Eventually though, as a result of this processing, I came to terms with all of what happened and am now no longer negatively affected by the event.

In directed abreaction, the therapeutic goal is to help a person re-live their experiences so they can put them into a contextual frame that makes sense to them, and in many cases resolve post-traumatic stress disorder, so they can function in healthy ways in today's world.

Although I do believe it is sometimes important or helpful for clients to understand the past, I do not believe they must re-live the past to get well. While understanding the past may make some changes easier (such as for recovering from PTSD), I do not think it is essential for change to occur - because truly, understanding the past is not a part of the change process; it is more of a tool for relapse prevention.

Related to this are two controversial issues in regard to clinical hypnosis. First is that memory is not like a tape recorder. It is flexible and does change over time. Things can be added or removed, and memory can be constructed. If used incorrectly, clinical hypnosis with age-regression can cause people to develop False Memory Syndrome, believing things occurred that did not, which can create many problems in the real world. Therefore, when doing all forms of regression or any work involving traumatic situations we must ensure we are properly trained and exercise extreme caution.

And then there is recreational abreaction. People are interested in being regressed back to a specific or general point in their past for various reasons. Some people want to re-experience emotionally-charged times from their life. Some believe in the concept of past lives, and want to explore the possibility. I do not advocate this practice, period.

The hypnotherapist must remember that whenever he uses a regression technique - of any kind for any purpose – there is always a possibility that the client will arrive at a highly emotional situation that causes them to suffer a strong and perhaps quite painful abreaction.

Personally, I fail to recognize much value in recreational abreaction, but you will meet individuals in psychotherapy who have histrionic or narcissistic personalities, and they sometimes seek out these experiences. Perhaps they believe that producing an intense emotion generates catharsis or relief, even though it doesn't bring them to a point of progress, but may instead simply reinforce their histrionic or narcissistic traits. Just be aware of this rare but real possibility, and proceed with caution. If you feel there is no therapeutic value to the abreactions, then do not proceed.

The ethical hypnotherapist always aims to avoid doing harm. Therefore, to intentionally cause abreaction with no therapeutic purpose in mind can be indicative of a poor assessment of the client's condition, or of attempting to treat a client with hypnosis when their psychological difficulties would best be addressed through referral to traditional counseling or psychiatric approaches.

So now we arrive at the obvious question: What do we do when abreaction occurs? First of all, if it is not related to the present problem, don't touch it. For example, when our client comes to us for smoking cessation and an abreaction occurs for whatever reason related to a prior traumatic experience, there is no therapeutic relevance to the presenting problem, and so we leave the issue alone. We refocus our client back on the task at hand, which in this case is a smoking cessation session.

Please know that rarely would a client experience abreaction during a smoking cessation session, as it is typically a reasonably simple process. However, if a client spontaneously abreacts during any kind of session, just instruct them, confidently, as if you were in total control and 100% calm and relaxed, that they are safe, they are well, the distressing scene is vanishing from their mind, and they are returning to this safe and comfortable office and towards addressing the issues at hand with you.

Second, never touch them. Let me repeat: Do not touch people who are abreacting. Leave them in their chair. If for some reason they flail around, try to keep them safe, move furniture if necessary, guide them gently to the floor if you have to, but really, really try not to touch them. Touching a client during abreaction can produce physical responses that are extremely stressful for them, and this may actually put us at risk, especially if the emotions are intense. And, touching a client during situations like this also opens doorways to liability-related issues.

There are some times in hypnosis where touching a client is appropriate, of course, such as a non-shaming, non-sexual, gentle touch on the shoulder, or perhaps touching their hand for emphasis is acceptable. However, you should always get informed consent early on, like during the pre-talk; "I may touch you on the arm during the session. If I do, it's simply to help you relax further. Will this be okay?" It is important to explain the purpose of our touch and to have them say it will be okay for you to do so. During an abreaction, however, never touch your client. That hard and fast rule is not meant to be broken.

Third, if you haven't experienced or witnessed an abreaction before, know that it will be tough for you, and it might even be scary. There's a commercial for an underarm deodorant that says, "Never let them see you sweat." Now is the time you hope you purchased a good antiperspirant, because a good hypnotist is able to remain in control.

Remaining calm and in charge during an emotional crisis is essential, so that we can move to the next step: We need to create a suggestion that brings our client back to the present.

A simple example is, "Bob, what you are experiencing right now is certainly difficult for you." (This is a pacing statement; it brings us into their reality, and eventually brings them back into ours. Using several of these is often helpful.) "We are going to move you into the present. It is now today. In today, you can look back to the events that you've experienced in life. Right now you are in my office. You are in my room. The events of the past are in the past. In the present, we are in my office. While we are in my office, we are taking a deep breath. We are relaxing. We are feeling safe. We are feeling secure. We are feeling at peace even with difficult things that happened in the past, which are not the present." This kind of brief script should help bring the client out of their traumatic mindset.

Be confident and use your common sense. Step firmly into your client's reality, direct them to release or let go of their negative, difficult emotions, and purposefully lead them back into the safety of the present.

Please note: If you are not a licensed mental health profes- sional - if you are only certified as a hypnotist - in many states, practicing directed abreaction as a part of hypnosis can be considered practicing psychiatry or psychology without a license, so if you have any inclination to engage in this kind of therapy, you should first consult your local laws and attain proper training and credentials.

Practice, Family and Referrals

It is easy to practice hypnosis on your friends and family. I encourage you to do some simple suggestions for relaxation and positive thinking, and maybe run through some hypnotic phenomena for entertainment purposes with anyone you can get to sit still long enough. This is a fun way to refine your skills and share hypnosis with those you care about.

By practice, I mean try and try and try again, with the goal of perfecting your patter and presentation style, because in reality, it can be really difficult to effectively hypnotize people you know, to actually attain high levels of trance for useful therapeutic sessions.

Your friends and family will generally see you as a friend and a family member, not as an authoritative professional, even when they know (or have at least been told) that you are one. They feel weird or silly having you hypnotize them, and may worry, despite your pre-talk, about divulging family secrets or whatever it is that people worry about. And this is why practicing on family and friends is very important and helpful: You learn to overcome challenges, build your confidence, and perfect your pre-talk – even if you never actually hypnotize those close to you.

Practice, practice, practice. Again, the more you go through the motions, recite inductions and form suggestions, the better you will become. Suggest that the fork now has the motivation it needs to work side-by-side with the knife to cut your pork chop. Suggest your car has the energy it needs to start and motor through the day. Explain the hypnotic process to an imaginary client while you're driving to work. You may drive everyone in your household and circle of friends crazy with this practice, but it will pay off as your skills are sharpened.

When practicing hypnotizing those we know, it is important to relax and have fun. If they laugh, laugh with them, but keep them focused. Be casual about the process – they will pick up on your calm confidence. And you must be confident. *Know* that you are the hypnotist.

Remember, however, that hypnosis only works when the subject is willing, so you cannot force your teenager to sit still on the couch for a session while you give them suggestions to clean their room and do their homework. Terror-based trance work does not work. Practicing with family and friends is truly for the purposes of perfecting your style and approach, formulating, adjusting and memorizing your patter, and becoming comfortable creating therapeutic suggestions.

That said, once you announce that you are a hypnotist and that you intend to help people lose weight, quit smoking, overcome their stage fright and so forth, and especially after you do a few successful demonstrations, you may find certain friends and family members coming to you for help with all sorts of issues.

Hypnosis for fun, practice and light issues is great with friends and family, but for serious, heavy duty issues, please refer people you know well to another professional. For one, you're not yet ready to handle heavy duty issues. And, the hypnotic process requires a specific level of trust between the client and the hypnotist. Strangers will come to your office without family or friend history or 'baggage,' and will leave your office without it, too. Traditional therapy has rules against "dual-relationships" - being friends with clients - and it is generally best to draw these lines with hypnosis as well, so as not to set up unhealthy, unequal or even unethical relationships with people you interact with in your real world.

And, until you are more experienced, please refer people you do not know who come to you with heavy duty issues, as well. Making referrals is one of the hallmarks of a good clinician. Recognize that we can't be everything to all people, and there are other competent professionals available.

In order to provide competent care, we must be competent. We must continually learn and practice and expand our skills and knowledge base, and this takes time. When a client calls for an appointment on an issue that you have not worked with before, do some research on the subject. Scour the Internet for ready-made scripts so you can study the suggestive approaches used by others. Call a hypnotist friend and ask their advice or opinion. This is how we learn.

And then make a decision. Do you feel comfortable, confident and competent to handle the issue with this client? Perhaps you do feel this way. But there is no shame in referring. Building a referral network is not only good business, but helps us to manage our liability and to do a good job.

Clinical hypnosis is one method of treatment for many conditions, but it is not always the best method for all conditions or all clients. You must be able to both recognize when another approach would be more beneficial for a client, and be able to refer them to an appropriate source for alternative therapy. It is helpful to network within your community and become familiar and friendly with available clinicians and agencies who provide services that you cannot or are not interested in providing, so that you are able to help your clients get the help they need, and so that they know you are out there and can refer hypnosis-ready clients to you.

CHAPTER 8

Hypnotic Phenomena

Just as every person is different and has different life experiences, every person will have slightly different experiences when under hypnosis, ranging from changes in reasoning, awareness and their creative imagination, to physical changes in blood pressure, heart rate, body temperature and other sensory perceptions. We refer to these changes as hypnotic phenomena.

Hypnotic phenomena are the bread and butter for stage hypnotists who demonstrate hypnosis for entertainment purposes. In clinical hypnotherapy, we will obviously not be demonstrating hypnotic catalepsy or amnesia for entertainment purposes, but we may explain and demonstrate some of these things for the purpose of convincing our clients that the hypnotic process is real and valid, so they can feel comfortable with the idea of hypnosis. If we are creative and open minded, we can learn, clinically, from stage hypnosis demonstrations.

I remember my first stage show as a hypnotist as if it happened yesterday. Because there is really no way to practice a stage show before you go live with it, you have to get it right the first time - but with no practical experience in stage hypnosis, it can be difficult to develop the confidence necessary to pull off that first show.

During the show, I suggested to a lady that she would forget the existence of the number 2. (This is a frequent stage demonstration, because not only can be quite humorous, it is simply amazing to witness, and a show is all about 'wowing' the audience.)

I told her to hold out her right hand, and count her fingers. She looked at me, looked at her hand, and counted: "1, 3, 4, 5, 6," then gave me a sheepish grin.

The audience was blown away - but so was I; it actually worked! I then had her hold out her other hand and count all of her fingers. She did and said, "1-3-4-5-6-7-8-9-10-11." With this, the crowd went wild, and I tried to conceal my own amazement.

After the show, still holding on to a little disbelief myself, I talked to her about her experience. She remembered little about the hour she spent on stage, and had clearly been in a deep trance state.

Of course I knew beforehand that demonstrating these kinds of hypnotic phenomena is how the hypnotist impresses and amazes the audience and creates entertainment, however, witnessing it as a participant and being the one to make it happen are two different things.

After I got over my shock that it worked so easily, I learned something from my experiences on stage: hypnotic phenomena is easy to produce, because even though these phenomena may seem odd or strange when isolated as a direct command on stage, they are actually natural extensions of life experience. Every manifestation of hypnotic phenomena occurs to one degree or another in real life.

For example, 'perceptual changes' are frequent hypnotic phenomena. The stage hypnotist uses this when they suggest to participants that they are freezing cold - and the group then instinctively huddles together in comical ways to stay warm. Mothers use this same phenomenon when their child bruises a knee, by suggesting that Mom can kiss the 'boo-boo' and make the pain go away. The athlete who hurts himself during the big game, but suppresses the pain so they can continue to do what is most important to them, essentially delaying the pain response until the final whistle, is practicing what can be considered hypnotic phenomena.

Singing and dancing like a rock star is a powerful stage demonstration of disassociation, but in real life, most of us depart in our mind from the stressors of the day to our daydreams, and students are notorious for creating alternate realities in their heads during college lectures.

The clinical hypnotist can use hypnotic phenomena to help clients in a variety of ways. Obviously, in medical situations, manifesting analgesia, anesthesia and ideodynamic responses can be useful. Helping a client take physical control of their body for panic disorder, test anxiety or nicotine withdrawal through disassociation, sensory perceptions, and other phenomena can be useful. Teaching test-takers, golfers and athletes how to create dual-realities can be of incredible performance value to them. Techniques of age-regression can help a person to resolve past difficulties by gaining new perspectives on their life events, and the phenomena of time distortion is a great stress management tool.

Now that I have more experience in hypnosis, I can understand the great precautions that a stage hypnotist must take in order to protect his participants, and I can also see the potential for abuse. However, unlike the professional associations who despise stage hypnotism, I still think that responsible demonstrations of hypnotic phenomena can actually enhance the entire field of hypnosis, including clinical hypnotherapy. I regularly attend stage hypnosis shows in Las Vegas and elsewhere, and often take my friends who are curious about hypnosis, because they can see the power of hypnotic phenomena; they see people having a good time and realize that hypnosis is not something to fear.

Hypnotic phenomena not only occurs on stage or in the therapy office, but also on a daily basis in regular life - we just don't notice these things going on. Sometimes we naturally experience time distortion. Have you ever been sitting through something that was really boring, and you start watching the clock, and time seems to move soooooo slowly, and it just drives you crazy? Or what about those times when you are so captivated by something that time just flashes by? The old cliché 'time flies when you are having fun' clearly demonstrates powerful, naturally occurring deep trance phenomena.

We naturally experience hypnotic amnesia - when we cannot remember a word that is on the tip of our tongue. We experience negative hallucinations - when we are looking all over for something only to find it has been in our hand or right in front of us the whole time. We experience 'highway hypnosis' when we drive - our mind is busy thinking about work or dinner or talking on the phone during the drive, and we don't realize that we are almost home until we pull onto our street.

Hypnotic phenomena includes: selective amnesia, muscular catalepsy, analgesia, anesthesia, disassociation, positive hallucination, negative hallucinations, sensory perception changes, time distortions, involuntary movement, perceptional changes, and establishment of a dual-reality. All of these are things that occur naturally in a person's life and can be used in the therapeutic process in a variety of different ways. The skill of a good hypnotist is to be able to direct and elicit these various phenomena at will, and utilize them for the specific goal or outcome of the client.

Muscular Catalepsy

This is perhaps one of the more interesting kinds of hypnotic state: all the muscles in a particular area of the body are balanced and rigid to the point where that arm or leg or hand is totally still and stuck, and cannot be moved. This phenomena is naturally pounced upon by stage hypnotists, who hypnotically glue people's hands to walls or arms in the air, but it can also have uses in the clinic.

Catalepsy occurs naturally in a variety of psychological and physical disorders ranging from schizophrenia to epilepsy, and can be utilized in the hypnotic process for a number of different reasons, especially if the physical issues that our client may have are related to irritable bowel syndrome, pain management, or post surgical recovery.

Analgesia

This is the dampening or absence of the sense of pain, without a loss of consciousness. Perhaps a dermatologist is removing a wart and the client is allergic to a local anesthetic. The anesthesiologist may use hypnosis and suggest to the patient that in the area where he is cutting the skin there is no pain, essentially mentally numbing the area. There is still some sensation and feeling that occurs, but even if the person sees the knife cutting into the skin and the wart being removed, there will be no sensation of pain. As with anesthesia, there is a general insensibility to pain, with or without the laws of consciousness, but anesthesia is primarily associated with profoundly deep levels of trance and total loss of sensation, not just pain.

Disassociation

This means simply separating oneself from an idea or experience by viewing it through a second or third person perspective, looking upon something that happened to you as if it happened to someone else. Disassociation in psychiatry has been given a rather bad rap, however I feel that if there has been a painful experience and my disassociation protects me from intense emotions and feeling traumatized, that is a good thing.

How is it that some people emotionally survive miserable situations like the Oklahoma City bombing or 9/11, when they experienced them firsthand? Through disassociation, the psychological process has kept them from feeling intense levels of pain that otherwise might be emotionally detrimental. Disassociation can be used in the hypnotic process to help our clients come to terms with their past and their ability to function today. I have always said, quoting from Chapter 449 in the *Big Book* of AA (Alcoholics Anonymous), that acceptance is the key to all of our problems today. Now, acceptance doesn't mean that I like the stuff that happened to me, it simply means that I am able to see it out there, look at it, and even though I don't like it, acknowledge that it exists, and then I can move from that point forward. This is a form of dissociation that our clients will find most valuable.

Positive Hallucinations

Positive hallucinations are very interesting. The 'positive' refers to mentally adding something to your scene or surroundings that is not really there. You see these in stage show demonstrations, such as when the hypnotist tells the participants that they are watching a scary movie, and then the participants will hallucinate that they are watching a scary movie and respond physically and emotionally to that movie. It's a perception of visual, tactile, auditory, gustatory and olfactory experiences, without any real external stimulus, and with a compelling sense of reality. This can be extremely well applied and noticed in visualization exercises.

Negative Hallucinations

This is a very powerful hypnotic phenomenon. Negative hallucination is when you are unable to see something which is in fact there. We all do this every day, blocking out the billions of bits of sensory data that would overload us if we focused on them. Right now, reading this, what are you not aware of? Despite that being a very hypnotic question, I am sure you can begin to tune into your surroundings and notice perhaps the whirr of some machinery, the site of the wall or roof, maybe the sound of birds or cars outside. You were negatively hallucinating these things because you were intently focused on reading. There is a famous case of a stage hypnotist who had a real live alligator walk right over participants who were lying down on the stage and due to the negative hallucination suggestions they received, they were totally oblivious to its presence. Amazing, but true.

Have you ever been making a sandwich, and you go to the refrigerator to get the mayonnaise out. You open up the refrigerator and you look for mayonnaise and you can't find it in there. You look all over for the mayonnaise. Finally you ask your spouse, "Hey honey, where's the mayonnaise? Are we out of mayonnaise?" And they walk right over, open up the door, and right there in front of your eyes is the mayonnaise.

What happened there? You had a negative hallucination. You gave yourself the suggestion when you were making a sandwich, "Hey, maybe we were out of mayonnaise," and then you acted on that suggestion. You opened the door, and you didn't see it, even though it was right there in front of you.

When we apply this to therapy, we have not only an extremely powerful convincer, but also a useful set of understandings, in that when we recognize what the client may previously have been negatively hallucinating in life, like for example people's positive reactions to them, we can point these out and allow them to truly enrich their world view.

Altered Sensory Perception

Our clients feel, taste, smell, hear, and see things differently when hypnotized than they do in a state of full alertness. This phenomena can be used to induce relaxation and is both a natural part of the hypnotic process and of our lives. For example, it's an average day and you go for a walk to simply get some exercise. As you are walking you notice that the sunset is beautiful. This is the first time during the day that you noticed the sky. The sky is quite beautiful. As you look at the sky, the visual senses that you experience become emphasized and increased and dominant at that particular moment. Your sensory perceptions have temporarily been altered to become primarily visual. When utilized in the hypnotic process, sensory shifts will almost automatically help to induce relaxation and deeper levels of trance, and responding physically to the hypnotic process.

Time Distortion

This is one of the most frequently occurring examples of hypnotic phenomena. I went to a group hypnosis event one day just to see what they were doing. It was a 'forty-nine dollars to quit smoking forever' session at a Holiday Inn. Even though I am no longer a smoker, I decided I would go see what this guy's 'show' was about. Two hundred people were there in a big banquet hall, and instead of sitting in chairs, he had everyone lying on the floor. For me this was marginally tolerable, however I am sure that some of the sixty-year-olds in the room found it impossible to be comfortable on the floor.

When the session was over, he asked the participants, "How long was that session? How many of you felt the experience was under three minutes?" A bunch of people raised their hands. I was shocked. He then asked, "How many of you believe the session was between three minutes and ten minutes?" About half the room raised their hand. And then, "If you think the session lasted for ten to fifteen minutes raise your hand." Most of the rest of the people raised their hands. And finally, "How many of you felt that the session lasted longer than fifteen minutes?" Out of two hundred people, there were maybe five or six hands up in the air. The majority of people thought it was less than ten minutes. He then pointed to the digital clock on the podium, to show that the session had actually been twenty-nine minutes long.

Like this guy, at the conclusion of my sessions I almost always ask my clients, "How did you feel when you were being hypnotized? Do you feel this was beneficial? Describe for me what you experience was like." One client said, "I felt like my body was really relaxed. I felt like I couldn't really move even if I wanted to. But my mind was sharp; I knew exactly what was going on the whole time." I then asked him, "How long do you think this session was?" He said, "Probably about ten or fifteen minutes." Clients almost always grossly underestimate the length of time. The session had run a little over thirty minutes. This frequently occurring phenomenon is, of course, an extremely effective convincer and demonstration of hypnotic power.

Involuntary Movements

These can occur naturally during the hypnotic process. During the induction or deepening I will say to clients, "You may notice a fluttering in your eyes. You may notice a trembling just beneath the surface of the skin. These are natural things that people sometimes sense or feel during hypnosis." When they note that they are experiencing those things, then they know they are experiencing hypnosis. Again, this also acts as a powerful convincer.

Ideo-dynamic or unconscious movements are another form of involuntary movement which we can utilize in hypnotherapy. These are those automatic or conditioned responses that are generated on an unconscious level by the subject in response to stimuli, either external or internal.

Unlike the other induced phenomena that we may experience while in trance, ideo-dynamic responses occur no matter what one does. There is literally no way the individual can prevent these unconscious body movements, or keep from re-experiencing feelings and sensations.

We can tell the client that their unconscious will lift a certain finger to answer a question with a yes, and another finger to answer a question with a no. We can then interrogate the client and ask them deep questions whilst gaining pure and uncensored information.

However, since ideo-dynamics are by definition unconscious responses, the greater the degree of dissociation present, the more that responses to feelings, movements or sensations suggested by the hypnotist can be enhanced. Therefore, facilitating dissociation is a necessary first step prior to attempting procedures such as automatic writing, or finger signaling.

There are three kinds of Ideo-dynamic Responses:
Ideo-affective, Ideo-motor, and Ideo-sensory.

Ideoaffective - Emotional Manifestations

Emotional manifestations are the automatic responses attached to the experiences of each individual. It is virtually impossible to be entirely devoid of feelings about something. Every person exhibits and attaches a wide range of emotional responses to various events in their lives, and these responses may differ in temperament and in the degree of intensity from person to person, and situation to situation. While in trance, the individual's feelings associated with the ideas contained in the hypnotherapist's suggestions may rise to the surface, such as buried negative feelings of hurt and despair, or positive feelings of joy and pleasure.

Ideomotor - Physical Manifestations

The body's unconscious reactions to one's thoughts are often referred to as Ideomotor Responses. This is also more commonly called 'body language'.

In therapeutic settings, the ideomotor response can be used to facilitate dissociation, to deepen the trance state, and as an indicator of responsiveness.

Idosensory - Sensory Manifestations

These are automatic mental experiences of sensation associated with the processing of hypnotic suggestions. The hypnotist will give a detailed description of the various sensory components associated with an experience, which allows the client to re-experience those sensations to a degree determined by the amount and type of past personal experience with it.

Phenomena such as hand levitation or lowering, such as in the sand bucket tests, are also examples of ideodynamic movement. When observing such responses to suggestion, be aware that smooth fluid and deliberate movement is not what we are after; we are looking for shaky, automatic and involuntary movement caused purely by their unconscious minds.

With hand levitation, one of their arms rising automatically as a result of both direct and metaphorical suggestion can be useful when piggy-backing other suggestions. For example, 'Now your right hand will begin to rise into the air, as if pulled up by a thousand helium balloons, light as a feather and lifting up higher and higher now. The higher this hand goes, the deeper into trance you go, and the more you respond completely at all levels to the beneficial suggestions you will soon be receiving."

Perceptual Changes

These powerful hypnotic phenomena occur not from the physical, but from the cognitive perspective. These manifest frequently in real life between mother and child. A three year old boy falls, scrapes his knee and starts to cry. What does Mommy do? She comes over and kisses the injury to make it feel better. Mom gives the suggestion that kisses make pain go away, then she kisses the boo-boo, the child smiles, shakes it off, and goes back to playing.

Hypnotic phenomena are interesting and perhaps amazing to witness, but they are still completely natural.

(Interlude)

Learning Hypnosis

Take a moment now to think about what you have learned in the past few chapters. What knowledge and skills have you already gained?

You know what hypnosis is, how to prepare people for it, how to induce the hypnotic state and deepen the process of hypnosis, how to craft effective suggestions and how to utilize various hypnotic phenomena for a specific target or goal, and how to awaken the client from trance.

Learning hypnosis through print can be a tricky issue, and it will require effort and energy on your part. With this book, Nathan and I are giving you the fundamental tools you need, but it is up to you to take this information into the real world and apply it.

I hope you have been practicing. If not, now is the time to begin! Explain how hypnosis works to the plant in the window. Recite an induction to your dog. Suggest to the microwave that every time it dings, it will feel cheerful and enthusiastic about a job well done.

Find ways and opportunities to practice hypnosis every chance you get. Perform simple inductions on friends and family, and demonstrate some hypnotic phenomena for the purpose of entertainment and fun. Hypnotize teddy bears, desk lamps and rocking chairs. Practice, practice, practice, again and again and again. And then, practice some more. Make sure that by the time you attempt clinical hypnosis with serious issues you are an experienced and competent hypnotist.

You may be reading this and thinking, "Nathan, Richard - you guys have been doing this for years, but how can you expect me to read one book and then get out there and start hypnotizing people?"

Well, first of all, we do not expect you to only read one book (although we do expect you to start practicing hypnotizing!) Learning how to do hypnosis is not something that can occur simply from reading a few pages or watching a few DVDs, or from a single weekend training course. Learning to practice hypnotherapy professionally will take lot of time and effort on your part. (And a lot of practice!)

If you feel overwhelmed by what you've read so far, take a break, break it down and re-read and practice short sections at a time.

There are many additional resources available for gaining more knowledge and understanding. We offer several training videos on a variety of single subjects, from induction and deepening approaches to hypnotic language to effective suggestive script writing. There are written scripts you can download and study, and audio scripts you can listen to and learn from. There are live training classes and online workshops and more textbooks and on and on and on. You will never be able to fully exhaust the educational opportunities available for improving your hypnosis skills.

The training process takes a great deal of time, and some would say that learning hypnosis a life-long journey. However, with practice, you already know enough now to actually take clients through some guided imagery and progressive muscle relaxation for induction and deepening, and to offer simple suggestions for positive change. Eventually, as you become more comfortable with hypnotic language and post-hypnotic suggestions, you will be able to incorporate those into the healing process.

It is helpful when you understand that performing simple hypnosis is not a big thing, especially since it happens daily, naturally, to everyone. You can easily start small and build up, so that you gradually take yourself from doing little induction and relaxation pieces to more powerful examples of hypnotic phenomena and instant induction.

When you are looking for friends and family to practice with, be light and respectful. Acknowledge up front that they may laugh or be nervous. You, however, should remain confident and relaxed. Take hypnosis seriously, but realize that when you are just practicing with people close to you, you can relax and have fun as well.

Practicing means trying, and trying means there is room for failure. You will fail. Sometimes your friend will simply not relax enough to give in and follow the induction process. Sometimes you will forget what you meant to say and lose trance. Sometimes your mother will not be able to stop laughing long enough to listen to your pre-talk. So what? This is how we learn. Usually you will easily be able to figure out why your last attempt failed, and therefore you can adjust your approach next time.

Just keep at it, keep practicing and keep hypnotizing. Before long you will amaze even yourself.

For additional basic and advanced training resources, please feel free to visit:

www.SubliminalScience.com

www.KeysToTheMind.com

CHAPTER 9

Applications and Cautions
- Memory and Age Regression

Memory Recall

Hypnosis for memory recall related to issues like test-taking anxiety and confidence building is highly effective. Generally, the problem is not with their memory at all, but with the worry – the anxiety and stress generated over possibly forgetting, which causes a panic-driven blocking effect. In this case, teaching the client how to relax and focus and think differently during testing situations can be quite beneficial for helping them to pass exams for which they have studied diligently.

However, there are some highly controversial issues in clinical and forensic hypnosis related to memory and recalling details of past events. One thing we have to understand is that memory, unlike a photograph, is not static. Memory is fluid and changes over time, and therefore it is not always 100% reliable. If the mind can't remember, the mind will fill in the blanks with its own creations.

External validation of what a client tells us in hypnotherapy related to past traumas or crimes is essential. This is the heart of the repressed memory issue from the 1980s and '90s, when several high profile cases about child sexual abuse, satanic ritual cults and other heinous crimes hit the court system, and in many of them, hypnosis was used to enhance the memory recall of the victims. As a result, convictions were made and then many were rescinded when it came to light that the memories elicited through hypnosis may have been false.

Repressed memory therapy is an area of tremendous liability for mental health professionals and hypnotists. When the elicitation of repressed memories turns out to be false or imagined, the resulting experience of "False Memory Syndrome" carries its own bunch of emotional and psychological ramifications. Today, anyone practicing repressed memory therapy with hypnotic methods is a sitting duck for lawsuits.

I want to stress that using forensic hypnosis to help recollect memories of known events (for example, robbery or rape) is acceptable, however, it must be done with (a) caution, (b) a recognition that memory is flexible, changeable, adaptable and not always accurate, (c) recognition that often times it cannot be used in court cases, and (d) a witness who has been hypnotized may not be allowed to testify at all.

Every jurisdiction has their own rules, which are, of course, subject to change at any time. Because of those high-profile cases a few decades ago, courts are now very skittish about accepting hypnotic memory recollections, because we know memory is not static. If a client believes that when under hypnosis they may be able to recall events necessary to testify, they must first seek other ways to verify the memories, and once memories are recalled, the validity of the details of the recovered event must be confirmed. Hypnotherapists should take care to make this a condition of "informed consent" in forensic hypnosis, and if someone comes to you for memory recollection services, you should have them check with their attorney first to see if it's really a good idea to proceed, or not.

There are a lot of cautions when it comes to the past. And, the real question in therapy is not what happened yesterday, but in what direction are we going, today? What skills need to be learned in order to move in that direction?

Age Regression and Age Progression

Age regression is different from repressed memory therapy, and is a totally appropriate and acceptable method of conducting hypnotherapy. Age regression is when, during the hypnotic process, we move our clients back to a point in life, maybe yesterday, maybe a month ago, maybe ten years ago, maybe even back to childhood, where they re-experience past events as if they were living them all over again.

Age regression can powerfully enhance memory. However, as we discussed before, it should be used with caution, as irresponsible age regression can cause abreaction or the creation of false memories. So, with these potentially negative responses, why would we ever want to use age regression at all?

Age regression is often used in certain therapeutic processes, like Elman's Hypnoanalysis, where one uses regression to "pin point" the cause or trigger of a problem, and the understandings drawn from the discovery help to resolve the issue. The key difference between regressions and memory retrieval is that when doing regressions, one experiences events first hand as if they are participating in the event in person for the first time, rather than just looking back and trying to recall pieces of an event. When used with all appropriate cautions, this is a very powerful way of gaining insight into the client's past times and experiences.

Regression can be elicited like any other phenomena through direct suggestions, metaphors, or a combination of both. For instance, after the induction and deepener, you might suggest, "Now we are going to move back in time to when you first experienced this problem. Going back now, through the days and the hours, time turning back, and when you arrive back at when you were experiencing this for the first time, let me know." You would then use simple questions such as, "Where are you now?" or, "How old are you?" and, "What can you see / hear / feel?" to orientate them to the scene, and then begin to question them on the actual mechanics of the problem itself.

There is also a hypnotic phenomenon called age progression. Not only we can go back in time and take a look, but we can also go forward in time. Now, of course we cannot predict the future, so what we mean when we talk about age progression is taking our attitudes, values, qualities, strengths, resources and attributes and applying them to a representation of a situation in the future. We can suggest that the client see themselves in the future breathing fresh air as a non-smoker, able to enjoy life without cigarettes, or without gorging themselves at a buffet, or whatever issue they are working on hypnotherapy.

Through suggestion, you can help the client apply the experiences and what they know about themselves today towards a perception of the future. The created image may not be accurate, because no one can know the future for certain, but a progression can create an emotional experience of using existing resources for problem-solving.

This is a useful and a valuable tool in hypnotherapy, and personally, I think age progression is probably under-utilized, whereas age regression is probably over-used.

Memory is at best a confusing issue, and at worst a dangerous one. Treat age regression and progression like any other hypnotic phenomena, but act with caution and care.

CHAPTER 10

Hypnotic Language

The structure and composition of the language that you use, and the way you craft and phrase your hypnotic suggestions at every part of the hypnotic process, is hugely important. Depending on how 'hypnotic' the language we use is, we can build agreement, shift the focus of attention, induce trance, embed suggestions, create binds or positive linguistic traps, and so much more, just with our choice of words.

The key influence in the hypnosis world's understanding and use of hypnotic language – the words we use and the way we use them during trance sessions – was Milton Erickson, who developed his language skills and ability of being 'artfully vague' to such an extent that he would often hypnotize and fully cure clients in a seemingly normal conversation, with the aid of hypnotic stories and metaphors.

When you learn hypnotic language and integrate it into every part of the hypnotic process, you will find the effectiveness of the hypnosis you do will increase 100 fold, as clients just naturally and automatically accept all the suggestions they receive.

In hypnotherapy, we try to help our clients generate a solution they agree with by the use of suggestions. Just like in traditional therapy, our goal is to move our clients to a point where they have that 'ah-ha' experience, and are able to immediately resolve their problems. Hypnotic language allows us to focus the resources of the mind in a specific way, whilst being 'artfully vague' enough for our clients to come up with their own solutions and resolutions that fit in perfectly with who they really are and what they really need.

We are going to overview several different language patterns that you will want to become familiar with. We could probably put together a three-hour lecture on each of these but in this text we will devote only a few paragraphs per pattern, and it will be up to you to do more research. A wealth of knowledge is available on the Internet and through instructional videos, books and training classes, and someone could probably develop an entire graduate school cur-riculum just on the hypnotic language patterns of Milton Erickson, many of which were identified, defined, broken down and studied by Bandler and Grinder when they created NLP, neuro-linguistic pro-gramming.

Language patterns help us to disassociate our clients from certain things, while focusing their attention on others. We want to be artfully vague, because we want to avoid disagreements with our client and allow them to come up with their own solution. After all, when it comes down to it, no one knows what a client really needs more than the client themselves. We are merely using the process of hypnosis to give them access to that knowledge.

Incidentally, hypnotic language is typically ascribed to indirect styles of hypnosis. We want our clients to build consensus with us. If a politician wants to succeed in debates or get his message across, then they would be well served by being artfully vague, using hypnotic language patterns and concepts of NLP. The more you learn about hypnosis and NLP, when you watch politicians speaking on television you will discover that most of the folks writing the speeches must have pretty strong backgrounds in both. The words will often be oxymoronic and specifically vague, because the politician's goal is to build consensus, rather than create divisions. He wants to avoid the use of anything that would bring out an objection.

Salespeople also find NLP useful. For example, instead of saying to a client, "Buy this red car," one might say, "And you know, as you come to consider which of the cars you will buy today, you may find yourself thinking about some cars that really catch your eye, and just how they will look sitting proudly in your own garage." As you learn the language patterns detailed below, think back to this brief example, and see if you can identify just why it was so hypnotic.

Another thing to bear in mind is that these patterns are also used by all of us, unwittingly.

In fact, you may notice your clients using some of these patterns themselves as they describe their problem to you, so you should keep an eye out for them and if you deem it necessary, stop your client and ask them to clarify; they may have used hypnotic language to hypnotize themselves into having their problem in the first place.

NLP has created a wonderful system called the 'Meta Model,' which describes how to deal with these accidental hypnotic patterns. Since this is not an NLP course we will not focus on these things here in great detail, however the Meta Model is certainly something that will be extremely useful for you to research.

Nominalization

Many successful motivational 'guru's are masters of nominalization. People who use NLP say any noun that cannot be put in a wheelbarrow is a nominalization. You can take a toaster and put it in a wheelbarrow, but you can't take learnings and put it/them in a wheelbarrow.

Learnings? Is that a word? Yes, it's a nominalization. You can make a nominalization out of any experience by turning it into a noun. In hypnotic language, you might say something like, "The learnings that you are experiencing..." Well, learnings is now a noun. It's a meaningless noun; it can't be put in a wheelbarrow. But using the word learnings forces our client to abstract what learnings are, and how they experience the sight, the sound, the touch of this new concept. The experience of learning will be up to the individual client. It's going to draw upon all of their sensory experiences. Nominalizations force our clients to draw on their wealth of experiences and resources and use these to really ascribe powerful and personal meaning to the words you use.

Three language patterns related to nominalizations are unspecified nouns, unspecified referential indices, and unspecified verbs.

Unspecified Nouns

Let's say I want a client to build consensus with me, to agree that hypnosis is a positive experience and would be beneficial to them. To accomplish this, I may say something like, "People successfully use hypnosis to get over their problems." Well, what people? Who are these people, and where are they? This statement is difficult for them to disagree with, because it uses an unspecified noun.

If I were to say, "Academics (a specific noun) use hypnosis to successfully solve problems," then someone might be able to disagree with that. Or, if I were to say, "Meghan uses hypnosis to improve the quality of her life," well, someone may be able to disagree or argue because it's tied to a specific person, not them. With an unspecified noun, however, listeners can only agree, thus building consensus.

Unspecified nouns help to avoid the subconscious conflicts that clients may create with specific nouns, whilst also causing them to accept your suggestions at some level. People can easily learn and understand how to use and apply these patterns in their communication, can't they?

Unspecified Referential Indices

These are nouns that really don't refer to anything, and are, in a sense, an example of unspecified noun. For example, "And a person can focus deeply on a certain sensation." This language patter is so vague as to both make disagreement virtually impossible, and leave the client room to manufacture for themselves the ideal sensation or experience.

Unspecified verbs

For example, "A person can enjoy this, easily..." Here the verb is 'enjoy,' however, the referential index of this verb is unspecified, so once again we are being artfully vague.

A person can see how these three patterns integrate and overlap, and enjoy thinking about how one could use them in a powerful and beneficial hypnotic process, and identify them when used accidentally by ones' clients, easily now, couldn't one?

Again, the purpose of hypnotic language is not to sound weird or strange, but to generate agreement and accept the client's subjective interpretation of what is said. Hypnotic language is all about creating a process for our clients that is in agreement with the suggestions we give them, and letting them interpret the words we use in the way that is most meaningful for them.

The clinician who watches stage shows can learn a great deal. Every skit builds upon the difficulty of the last, because consensus is built by the stage performer throughout the show from skit to skit. In hypnotherapy, we want to build consensus with our clients. Using hypnotic language in our scripts is one way to accomplish this goal, and as I am sure you are beginning to notice, it also has many other benefits.

Three other language patterns that are important for us to know are complimentary adjectives and adverbs, the use of comparable statements and a process called mind reading.

These three patterns are keys to hypnotic language because they create agreement and help to disassociate our clients from things we don't want them to focus on, while also applying their energies in the directions that we want them to go.

Complementary Adverbs and Adjectives

The basic concept of high-end complementary adverbs and adjectives is to use two complementary adjectives together in the same sentence, thereby encouraging clients to accept our presuppositions. In the example, "Easily experience the pleasures of self-discovery," easily and pleasure are complimentary adjectives and adverbs, which reinforces, through high content levels, the presupposition that we want our clients to accept.

What we are presupposing in this sentence is that our clients will experience self-discovery, and that this experience will be pleasurable. When you craft sentences which presuppose a certain fact, acceptance of this fact will be beneficial to the client. Presuppositions can be very basic: 'when you quit smoking;' or more covert: 'when you look at yourself in the mirror in a few weeks time and realize that you are a non-smoker, just how big will your smile be?' In both examples, the presupposed fact is that the client shall quit smoking. Using com-plimentary adjectives can ensure these presuppositions are accepted without challenge or debate.

Comparable Statements

Comparable statements are used to build consensus, create disassociation, and draw our clients into what we want them to focus on. Comparable sentences use the word 'as' to link suggestions together, one of which is usually accepted as a presupposition, while the other draws the focus of the mind. For example, "You will feel good as you notice your weight dropping dramatically."

Mind Reading

This is where we assume knowledge that could only really be gained through mind reading. For example, "I know that you have chosen to make the changes which I have suggested." Mind reading is an interesting way of gaining authority of proof in the mind of the client (if your 'mind reads' are vague or accurate enough to be accepted), and also a subtle way of implying suggestions.

Cause and effect patterns, also known as linguistic bridges or linkages are also very powerful.

The mind likes to draw bridges and make connections between ideas, and has also been shown to act more powerfully on suggestions when given a reason, no matter how irrational the reason is. The suggestion 'notice as the sound of my voice causes you to relax deeply' has no logical basis; however you'll find that it will generate a much more powerful response than simply telling your client to 'relax.'

Other **powerful words you can use when linking ideas** are *and, as, which means, which causes, allows, enables,* and *encourages.*

Because you are reading this book the information you are learning causes you to think deeply about how you can use and apply these patterns in the hypnosis you do, which means that as you enjoy this book you are becoming a much more confident and effective hypnotist.

Do you remember the old TV show *School House Rock* with the song 'Conjunction Junction, What's Your Function?' They talked about language – verbs, pronouns, adjectives, conjunctions and such - and pre-sented a little educational clip between the cartoon clubs. The words 'and' and 'but' are examples of a **conjunction.**

As you sit here and relax, realize conjunctions are used to draw comparisons that our clients can agree with, and are a very powerful way of using cause-effect patterns. Like linguistic bridges, conjunctions can be useful for building agreement.

Connections and time are important.

Connections and time let our client build consensus not only with the present, but an agreement with the presuppositions and the suggestions that we are making for the future. This is one of the reasons why post-hypnotic suggestion is effective. It is easy for my client to agree with, "I am not smoking right now," because they are sitting in your non-smoking office. For my client to take it from the office, seven days out, ten days out, thirty days out, sometimes requires that they accept the suggestion post-hypnotically, and making a temporal connection allows this to happen. "As you hear these words, you become curious about your abilities." The phrase 'as you hear these words' is a time relationship. *As I hear these words, I become curious about my abilities. As I become curious about my abilities, I can extrapolate that into time.* Now we are actually into age progression, even on a non-level scale.

If this last pattern is a little confusing, don't worry. It can be much more simply applied, and is often called 'time distortion.' For example, we can take our clients forward into the future with quite direct suggestion, such as, "See yourself in the future as a non-smoker," or we can use time distortion to create a powerful 'future memory' in the mind of the client: "And imagine yourself in the future, a few weeks from now as a non smoker, looking back on now as being the start of a wonderful positive change."

If we wish to take this to an even more hypnotic level and introduce a confusion element (confusion is incredibly useful for both lowering of resistance and aiding the acceptance of suggestions), we might continue with this suggestion by saying, "And allowing your mind to drift still further into the future, to 3, 4, 5, 20, 30 years in the future, seeing yourself remaining confidently smoke free, and with each new year looking back with pride at the past, and looking forward with pride to the future." Notice how creating these connections in time are powerful and effective at planting long-lasting, self-reinforcing and time-resistant hypnotic suggestions.

Clichés and Adages

'Too many cooks spoil the broth.' Well, according to whom? Who made this judgment? This is a powerful way of being motivational and seeming to speak from a place of authority, such as, "It is important that you relax deeply now, and allow me to help you, because many hands make light work." In this example, two lost performatives were combined with the conjunction 'because' to create a reasonably hypnotic suggestion. It is good to learn these patterns, use them, and look for them in the natural speech of your clients.

Conversational Postulates

Conversational postulates are requests for action phrased in a yes or no sentence. For example, "Can you answer the phone?" To reply to this yes or no question with a yes or no answer would be facetious, because we can clearly identify these as imperatives hidden in question form. In the induction or the deepening, you may say to the client, "Can you go deeper into trance at this moment? Can you keep your eyes closed? Can you create in your mind a mental picture that brings you peace and serenity?" This is a request for action.

Let's say we're working with a client for weight loss. We could suggest, "Can you start eating smaller portions?" Or, "As you see yourself moving through the buffet line, you experience the desire to eat smaller portions and to only to take in enough food to meet your essential needs for nutrition. Can you do this?" Again, it's a request for action based on a yes or no question.

These conversational postulates are useful for building consensus, for disassociating our clients from the things we don't want them to focus on and associating with things we do want them to focus on during the hypnotic process. It is also a nice and non-demanding way of issuing instructions that we all use on a daily basis. *Can you learn these patterns easily and naturally?*

Lost performatives, also called indirect pre-suppositions, are language patterns containing at least one judgment, whilst leaving the source of the judgment ambiguous.

Presuppositions

Presuppositions are statements which can only be accepted and processed by the client if they unconsciously accept a particular suggestion to be true, and therefore they are an extremely effective method of suggestion giving.

There are many types and forms of presuppositions, one of which is temporal, or time based. A client may hear distracting noises during the induction, and you may suggest that those noises will simply reinforce their experience of relaxation. This is a common presupposition told with a time orientation to help them incorporate the experiences into the hypnotherapy, rather than to disassociate from the hypnotherapy process because of the noises that they hear.

As you read this book there may be other things happening around you, but it is interesting to notice that as the rest of the world continues around you, your focus on these words only continues to deepen and intensify as you are learning easily now.

Ordinals

Presuppositions may also be based on ordinals, which are the words first, second, third, fourth, fifth and so on. For example, "As you relax, you can first take a deep breath. Second, relax all of your muscles, and third close your eyes." With this example, relaxation is presupposed as specific manifestations of relaxation are given.

Ordinals can also be used in our suggestive process to cause our client to create an agreement. In the context of smoking cessation you may suggest, "The first thing you can do is make a decision.

You've already made that decision or you wouldn't be here today. Second, you can begin to focus on your body. As you feel your body, the sensations that you are currently experiencing are sensations of peace and satisfaction, because you know that you have made the right decision. Third, from this point forward, you will consider yourself to be a nonsmoker not because you are going to do something in the future, but because it is what you have already become."

First, second, and third—they presuppose an order of things and implied instruction. *First you are going to read these words, second you are going to think about what you have learned, third you are going to begin practicing it in the real world, fourth you are going to find yourself getting really good at hypnosis, fifth you will then find yourself being an accomplished and successful hypnotist.*

The Choice of "Or"

The word 'or' is itself presupposition; "Would you prefer to continue to breathe in carbon dioxide with each breath, or would you rather breathe in fresh air?" This example gives our clients an obvious choice and builds consensus, because it gives them a choice of only two things - one of which they know that they don't want to do, and one they know they do want to do. The word 'or' is a presupposition as it presupposes that there are only two available options.

Awareness

'Have you realized that it is easy to go into hypnosis now?' 'Notice how you are relaxing?' 'Are you aware just how quickly you are accomplishing your goals?' These statements all require you to accept that what is being presupposed is true. People will naturally accept what you are asking them to realize or notice, because the issue for them becomes not whether what you suggest is true or not, but whether they have realized or noticed it occurring or not.

Have you realized just how easy awareness presuppositions are to use and apply?

Binds

A great pattern to use is the bind, an example of cause and effect, which causes people to be linguistically bound or trapped in a continual loop. For example, "The more you hear my voice, the more you feel relaxed." This can also be extended: "The more you hear my voice, the more you relax, and the more you relax, the more you realize just how good it feels to go into hypnosis, and the deeper you go the better you feel, the better you feel the deeper you go."

Double Bind, or Illusion of Choice

This is often used poorly by sales people who might say something like, "Would you like this car in red or green?" with the presupposition being that you like the car. In hypnosis, we can be much more subtle and elegant. Milton Erickson would often ask his clients, "Would you like to go into a trance in this chair or that chair?"

When you think about and practice these patterns, it becomes quite easy to invent them on the fly to fit almost any situation. "Will you find yourself emerging from this trance feeling happy, positive and energized, or will you simply find yourself feeling as if you have had one of the deepest and most rewarding nights of sleep in your life?"

And I don't know whether you will learn these patterns easily and begin going out there and practicing talking hypnotically at once, or whether you will just find yourself naturally using these patterns more and more in your everyday communication without even having to think about it.

Embedded Commands

"People can *go into a trance* deeply, and as you *go into a trance* realize just how easy it is *to enter trance now*." The command parts of the sentence can be absorbed by the unconscious mind separately from the rest of the communication, and subconsciously acted upon. Embedded commands are much more powerful if subtly marked out, either with a shift in tonality, a subtle gesture or mannerism, or something else only just noticeable. Practice ways to use embedded commands in your speech, and notice just how powerful they can be.

Ambiguity

Exploiting the ambiguous meaning of words can both induce confusion and subtly embed commands. There are many types of ambiguity: phonological, such as the old sales example "by now" being used as an embedded command for 'buy now,' and with punctuation (or lack thereof), where the beginning of one sentence and the end of another overlap, often utilizing phonological ambiguity, such as: 'and you will wonder just what will be*come successful now.'*

Ambiguity can also be based on scope: 'speaking to you as someone who likes to experience hypnosis.' Here the scope is unclear, as it could be either yourself or the client who is the person mentioned.

Experiment playing around with the various ways words, sentences and phrases can be interpreted. *And speaking to you as someone who loves hypnotic language patterns are easy to learn it is quite natural to see how you can put these ideas into practice.*

There are too many patterns and ways of speaking hypnotically to enumerate and list, so for now just focus on the ones we covered above, practice them, explore them and learn them. Search for the 'Milton Model' on the Internet for more examples and resources if you feel you need them, and if you are really serious about truly mastering these patterns, buy the book "Patterns of the Hypnotic Techniques of Milton H Erickson, M.D., Volume 1," by Richard Bandler and John Grinder.

So begin to find yourself easily absorbing these patterns easily now and notice just how quickly you find yourself practicing, and realize that the more you practice the better you get because when you practice you will either find yourself confidently spinning patterns like a hypnotic master, or simply observing the amazingly hypnotic effects you words seem to have on others.

CHAPTER 11

Clinical Applications of Hypnosis - Therapeutic Intervention

In this section I want to give you a little bit of clinical evidence showing that hypnosis is effective, and also offer up a few of the cautions and considerations you should observe when creating intervention in these areas.

Again, it is important to realize that hypnosis is not a one-size-fits-all treatment. Some clients do require a referral for variety of reasons, and some problems will be either beyond the scope of your personal skills or hypnotherapy in general. It is therefore very important for hypnotherapist to be skilled in both assessment and referral.

We will begin with a discussion on hypnotizing children, and then move on to the most common conditions and disorders you may find in your office.

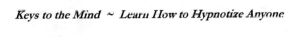

Hypnotizing Children

I am often asked if we can do hypnotherapy with children, and the answer is yes, most definitely. Interestingly enough, many stage hypnotists prefer working with teens and young adults over older adults, because they make such excellent subjects. Children are in the middle of the most exciting time of experience in life. The five senses of sight, sound, touch, smell and scent are more open and emphasized in a child's life - not polluted by experiences or limitations – and therefore the hypnotic process, which draws on sensory experiences, is easy to accomplish with children.

Children have vivid imaginations and are able to create clearly defined mental images as we talk to them in the hypnotherapy process. Also, children are not jaded by skepticism. They view us as an authority and accept what we tell them – if for no other reason that we are older, and perhaps because we have a title: hypnotist.

You may find it interesting that the critical factor (gate keeper between conscious and subconscious minds) is not really developed until we reach the age of about 7 years old.

My eldest children, Ricky and Rachel, have always been pretty good about going to sleep at night. My youngest child, Alex, on the other hand, is another story. He likes to stay up late and does not like to wake up in the morning - much like his father. One night when Alex was probably 5 or 6 yrs old, I was busy trying to finish an important project and Alex was having a hard time getting to sleep. From down the hall I would hear, "Daddy?" Sigh. "Yes, Alex, what is it?" "Get me some water?" I'd go get him water and head back to my office. "Daddy, turn the light on in the hall." I would turn the hallway light on, go back, sit down, and a little while later I'd hear, "Daddy, come read to me." He just wasn't going to sleep. This went on for about 30-45 minutes, and I was up against a deadline.

I was frustrated. He wanted me to stay and talk to him, but I just couldn't because I had to work on my project. And suddenly I had an idea: "Look, I really can't sit here and talk to you anymore because (a) it's really late and you are supposed to be asleep, and (b) I have to finish something. However, I have a relaxation cassette tape in my office. It's me speaking. Would you like to hear that?" He said, "Sure," so I got the tape and set it up in his room. I told him, "You don't have to just listen to me talk, you can also do the things that I ask you to do on the tape, if you want to."

He was only 5 or 6 years old at the time, but he seemed kind of excited to hear dad on tape. He snuggled down closed his eyes and listened, and I backed out of the room. The recording was a typical complete progressive muscle relaxation session with breathing exercises and visualization. I went back to my office figuring in a few minutes I would hear, "Hey dad, turn this off," or "Hey dad, this is weird," but no. After about ten minutes I poked my head in the door and there was Alex lying on the bed, actually tensing and relaxing his muscles, following the instructions on the progressive muscle relaxation tape. As I watched in awe, he drifted off into deep sleep.

The next night when I was tucking him in I asked, "Hey, did you like listening to that tape last night?" He said, "Yeah, it was cool." (Dad's cool, yea!) I was almost afraid to ask, "Would you like to hear it again?" but I did. He said, "Sure," so I turned it on and he was out like a light. Now, several years later, whenever Alex has trouble going to sleep he digs out the CD version of the PMR session and plays it. He enjoys the exercises, the breathing and visualization.

Kids are open-minded and once exposed, most become big fans of hypnosis. They can relate to our examples of 'zoning out in class' and understand that it's a naturally occurring phenomenon; there is nothing mysterious about it to them. They are at the natural phase in life where they are learning to take physical control over their bodies as well as creative control over their minds anyway, and so the concept of hypnosis fits right in.

Dave Elman, when working with children under the age of 10, would spend only about 30 seconds on the complete pre-talk, induction and deepening phase of the hypnotic process, and from there he would immediately move on to suggestion-giving. He did this by facilitating what he called the 'pretend game,' where he would simply say, "Close your eyes and pretend that they are glued shut. Now test them. Now pretend that you can't remember your name. Now relax yourself completely and pretend that you are in deep, deep hypnosis." And that's all it took. When working with children, keep it fast and fun. Do not bore them with long inductions unless you actually do want them to fall asleep.

I have seen teens for text-taking anxiety and memory recall during exams, for sports performance, for weight loss issues and for confidence and self-esteem. It is easy to take children from a normal waking state to the experience of profound deep trance phenomena like amnesia and hallucination in a matter of minutes or even seconds, because they are already there, ready to accept and fully act on your suggestions, as long as it is fun, fast, rewarding, pleasant, and their imagination is stimulated.

Personally, I do not work with children under age 15 or 16, for no real reason other than with experience we discover that we each work best with certain kinds of clients, and I feel that I am more effective with older teens than younger children. Obviously, you should never practice hypnosis with children of any age without first gaining the permission and consent of their parents. And, a rule I have that you should consider following as well for liability reasons is to always insist on at least one parent being in the room during the session if the client is under 18.

Research indicates that pediatric hypnosis is effective:

> ➤ **Hypnosis in pediatrics: applications at a pediatric pulmonary center**

By Ran D Anbar, Associate Professor of Pediatrics and Medicine, Department of Pediatrics

Upstate Medical University, 750 E. Adams Street, Syracuse, NY 13210, USA

BMC Pediatrics 2002, 2:11   doi:10.1186/1471-2431-2-11

• *Background*

This report describes the utility of hypnosis for patients who presented to a Pediatric Pulmonary Center over a 30-month period.

• *Methods*

Hypnotherapy was offered to 303 patients from May 1, 1998 – October 31, 2000. Patients offered hypnotherapy included those thought to have pulmonary symptoms due to psychological issues, discomfort due to medications, or fear of procedures. Improvement in symptoms following hypnosis was observed by the pulmonologist for most patients with habit cough and conversion reaction. Improvement of other conditions for which hypnosis was used was gauged based on patients' subjective evaluations.

- *Results*

Hypnotherapy was associated with improvement in 80% of patients with persistent asthma, chest pain/pressure, habit cough, hyperventilation, shortness of breath, sighing, and vocal cord dysfunction. When improvement was reported, in some cases symptoms resolved immediately after hypnotherapy was first employed. For the others improvement was achieved after hypnosis was used for a few weeks. No patients' symptoms worsened and no new symptoms emerged following hypnotherapy.

- *Conclusions*

Patients described in this report were unlikely to have achieved rapid improvement in their symptoms without the use of hypnotherapy. Therefore, hypnotherapy can be an important complementary therapy for patients in a pediatric practice.

> *Complementary and Alternative Medicine: A Focus on Hypnosis in Children and the Integrative Treatment of Atopic Dermatitis*

By Tammy C. Tempfer, MSN, RN-C, PNP

- *Indications for Hypnosis in Children*

The indications for hypnosis include patient motivation and a problem that is potentially treatable with hypnosis. The patient needs to be motivated to remedy the problem, and a good rapport must exist between the patient and the clinician.

Numerous pediatric problems have been successfully treated with hypnosis, including anxiety associated with procedures or illness, asthma and allergies, enuresis and encopresis, and habit disorders like smoking, tics, nail biting, and thumb sucking. It has been used to enhance self-esteem and self-confidence, and for sports enhancement, sleep problems, and attention deficit disorders. Hypnosis has also been successfully applied to enhance surgical anesthesia and ease discomfort during dental procedures.

Intervention Efficacy

When people ask me if hypnosis is effective, I tell them, "Hypnosis is effective for those who hypnosis is effective for." I believe the research, and the research shows that people with medical problems, emotional problems and undesirable habits can overcome their difficulties using hypnosis. I believe it is a preferred modality of treatment in many cases and for most clients, because it is natural, and it is primarily a form of brief therapy. In today's world of limited time and resources, brief therapy is a preferred method.

But again, hypnosis is only effective for those who it is effective for. Only quacks believe that only one modality of treatment always works and is effective for everything and everyone.

I know many chiropractors, some who even practice hypnosis. One of these friends had orthoscopic surgery on his injured knee, and he did not reject traditional surgical procedures to deal with his orthopedic condition. Most chiropractors are not quacks. They use chiropractic medicine as a conservative treatment to avoid invasive procedures, but most chiropractors will certainly refer to a surgeon or other medical doctor when necessary.

However, I have also met a few chiropractors who *are* quacks. They believe that all human disease, pain and suffering is in the spine, and they detest traditional medicine. They think adjustments can cure everything from ear infections to cancer and psychiatric difficulties, and they never make referrals.

(Out of fairness to my chiropractor friends, in my opinion, some MDs - who believe (or at least practice as if) medication is the cure to all human difficulties - are quacks too. We know, for example, that exercise three times a week is more effective than psychotropic medication for the treatment of major depression, yet many doctors will automatically write a prescription for pills instead of helping the client develop an appropriate exercise regimen. Why? The pill approach is simply faster and easier for the doctor. When I asked an anesthesiologist why he does not use hypnosis during childbirth, his reply was honest: "I can make $1400 in five minutes giving an epidural, or $100 doing a forty-minute hypnosis session. You do the math.")

Different things work for different people, and research proves that hypnosis works for a lot of people. However, it is not something to apply indiscriminately to all clients for all conditions. Sometimes hypnosis is the better choice, and sometimes it is not. For those clients who are willing to learn new skills and seek brief intervention via a natural approach with demonstrated efficacy, hypnosis is effective and should be considered a first-line intervention, rather than relegated to the back of the clinician's repertoire.

➢ *Hypnosis in Contemporary Medicine*

By James H. Stewart, MD   Mayo Clin Proc. 2005;80:511-524

Hypnosis became popular as a treatment for medical conditions in the late 1700s when effective pharmaceutical and surgical treatment options were limited. To determine whether hypnosis has a role in contemporary medicine, relevant trials and a few case reports are reviewed. Despite substantial variation in techniques among the numerous reports, patients treated with hypnosis experienced substantial benefits for many different medical conditions. An expanded role for hypnosis and a larger study of techniques appear to be indicated.

And now one more time before we get into heavy discussion, let us again hash over giving suggestions via hypnosis scripts. Many hypnosis books or courses will provide you with scripts - word for word exactly what you should say when doing hypnosis, from the pre-talk through to the awakening. As mentioned earlier, we recommend that if you come across scripts, feel free to read and learn from them, study the language used and the way the suggestion works, and if you really must, practice with them, but whenever possible try not use them with real clients. Your attention should be on the client, not on a piece of paper in front of you.

You want to watch your client, to study their reactions. You want to be able to flow with words and ideas naturally, and allow your mind to tell you what is best to do in the moment.

Milton Erickson tells a story about when he was a child. He had a job trying to get a local pig farmer to buy or sign up for something, and the farmer was quite reluctant and uncooperative. As he was talking to the farmer, young Milton bent down and began to scratch one of the hogs that was milling around next to him in the barn. The farmer, observing the way the hog relaxed and responded to this scratching, said, "You know what kid; I'll sign up because you know how to scratch a hog."

Erickson didn't know that this was going to happen when he started scratching the hog, he just found himself reacting instinctively or subconsciously. When working with clients, you want to trust your unconscious and have faith in your ability to come up with wonderful, powerful and deeply meaningful suggestions, phrases, metaphors and even original inductions and deepeners – right now, in the moment. Just practice and you will soon find this skill coming naturally.

And now, moving on to conditions and treatment. We have divided up the common issues you will be working with into five categories:

- **Behavioral Issues**
- **Psychiatric and Emotional Issues**
- **Pain Management**
- **Sexual Issues**
- **Stress Management**

Behavioral Issues

Hypnotherapy is often used as the modality of intervention for four primary behavioral issues: smoking cessation, weight loss, general habit control, and drug and alcohol withdrawal.

Smoking Cessation

Smoking cessation is probably the most prevalent use for hypnosis. Why does hypnosis work for smoking cessation? It works because it changes the subconscious associations that the smoker has with cigarettes. For twenty years, every time they get in a car, they light a cigarette. Every time they get angry, they light a cigarette. These are subconscious associations, habits. The conscious mind learns through repetition; it repeats the experience of cigarette after cigarette and connects them to various specific triggers, be they situations, emotions, locations or actions. Many smokers report that after they quit, they still reach for cigarettes in their purse or front pocket. These people have quit without hypnosis. Appropriate hypnotherapy for smoking cessation will change these automatic associations and behavior patterns.

Hypnosis is also effective because helps a person manage the physical effects of withdrawal. Hypnosis in and of itself can be an alternative coping strategy. Hypnosis removes a very large part of the cravings associated with smoking, and also helps deal with the secondary gain. As mentioned earlier, people smoke for a reason – perhaps to feel more confident or maybe they think it relaxes them or makes them look cool. With hypnosis, you can allow them to find within themselves the benefits or resources they think smoking gives them, therefore eliminating the need for cigarettes.

The evidence is fairly clear in saying that nicotine gum and patches and other forms of nicotine replacement therapies are highly ineffective (by themselves) compared to hypnosis, as they fail to address the psychological aspects of smoking mentioned earlier. With hypnosis, we can generally eliminate every single one of their reasons for smoking whilst dealing with learned triggers, associations and habitual behaviors and greatly reducing cravings. All people are different of course, and certain approaches may work better for certain clients.

Why it works:

The mind is interesting; it is like a computer, remembering everything that we do and creating automatic behaviors out of mundane life experiences. Without reprogramming these automatic associations, quitting smoking can be a difficult task. However, with hypnosis, changing these automatic behaviors is possible; the old associations are erased in the computer of our mind, and the new and healthy patterns are committed to the subconscious.

Evidence that it works:

Researchers at Texas A&M University System Health Science Center College of Medicine reported 81% of patients referred to hypnotherapy for smoking cessation reported they were smoke free at the conclusion of a three-session treatment program.

~ 48% reported they were smoke free at the end of a year.

~ 95% reported they were satisfied with the treatment they received.

The Dana Farber Cancer Institute in Boston found, "These results suggest that hypnotherapy may be an attractive alternative smoking cessation method, particularly when used in conjunction with a smoke-free worksite policy that offers added incentive for smokers to think about quitting."

In a study of the American Lung Association of Ohio Hypnotherapy Smoking Cessation Program, it was found that only 20% of clients prescribed nicotine replacement therapies were compliant and that "Hypnotherapy smoking cessation treatment offers an alternative cessation method, which may meet the unique needs of certain individuals."

In the Ohio study, a randomly selected sample of participants completed telephone interviews up to 15 months after attending a treatment session. Twenty-two percent of participants reported not smoking during the month prior to the interview.

Cautions:

Many hypnotherapists use aversion therapy to accomplish smoking cessation. They suggest 'whenever you see a cigarette you will feel totally repulsed and get a horrible taste in your mouth' or other such negative suggestions. This can be effective in some cases, but I feel because it is essentially a very unpleasant modality and one which creates a great deal of internal conflict for the client, and therefore torment and anguish should only be used as a last resort. It is far better to fully eliminate the need and desire to smoke from a person's conscious and unconscious mind, enabling them to become a healthy smoke-free individual. Otherwise, if we do not address the physical cravings and needs met, for example, the client may decide that a nasty taste is worth the social benefits smoking. Your clients will be more successful with positive live-changing suggestions.

Additionally, suggestions (both when awake and under hypnosis) to utilize adjunct relapse prevention supports (Nicotine Replacement Therapies, call a friend, breathe deeply, exercise, etc) are may increase efficacy.

Weight Loss

Hypnosis helps with weight loss. Only one strategy will help a person to succeed at both losing weight and keeping it off, and that is to expend more calories than you take in each day. Most of us have tried losing weight through traditional methods of dieting and exercising, and these kinds of programs are often scientifically effective. Fad diets, like eating nothing but grapefruit or cutting out carbohydrates, can help a person to reach a quick weight-loss goal. However, without a plan for maintaining your motivation and weight once you achieve your initial goals, no matter how you got there, you will quickly find yourself right back where you started.

The real reason people fail at weight loss is not the ineffectiveness of the diets, but rather the failure that people on diets have with changing lifelong patters of thinking. There is no such thing as a "Hypnosis Diet." Hypnosis is an effective tool for promoting weight loss because it can do what diets cannot: It can help you reprogram the destructive associations you have with food and re-frame your vantage point on exercise and physical fitness, helping you to change your overall lifestyle.

Conscious approaches to learning, like positive affirmations or cognitive therapy, can certainly play a role in helping a person to achieve weight loss, and learning specific strategies for diet, nutrition and exercise are all valuable tools. But research now shows that the subconscious mind controls much more of our behaviors than previously thought.

The subconscious mind controls muscle movement, heart rate, breathing and the autonomic nervous system. It is powerful, and quickly commits to habit what it learns. We were not born knowing how to walk, but over time, we learned. Watch any toddler and you can see them trying to remember how to take the next step. By the time a child can run, they no longer think about how to take the next step - they just do it.

We have no doubt committed to memory unhealthy patterns of eating, such as unconsciously associating bread with butter and salad with dressing. If you are on a diet, you struggle to make con-scious choices based on the recommendation of the diet. But when you are off the diet, the unconscious kicks in and tells you to put frosting on your brownie, without ever thinking about the impact on your diet.

Many of us grew up hearing our parents tell us to eat everything on our plate and not to be wasteful. Now, when we go into a restaurant that wants to convince us we have received a good value for our money by serving us portions that are three to four times larger than the recommended caloric intake, we subconsciously choose to eat everything they serve us, even if it is self-defeating and unhealthy.

There is much more to weight loss than simply dieting or exercise. The subconscious relationships we have with food are just as powerful as our conscious behaviors. In essence, you could say that it is possible to think yourself thin - because if we change these subconscious associations, we are able to choose a healthy manner of living automatically.

People are often surprised to learn that they can alleviate lifelong phobias and fears with neuro-linguistic programming, a modality of psychology that quickly transforms our subconscious perceptions of events through creative visualization. People are equally surprised to learn that clinical hypnosis is a highly effective way of achieving life goals. Both methods, which often overlap in some ways, can help you to make significant life changes if you choose to learn the principles of change.

The following unconscious misbeliefs often keep people who are trying to lose weight from achieving their goals:

- If it looks weird, green, or like a vegetable, it must taste bad.

- If it is good for me, it must taste terrible.

- If it is bad for me, it must taste good.

- Food brings me emotional satisfaction.

- I must eat everything on my plate.

These kinds of misbeliefs are often ingrained into our sub-conscious. Sam-I-Am's friend did finally try the green eggs and ham, but it took a lot of coaxing. Hypnotic suggestion could have saved Sam a lot of distress and changed his little friend's subconscious associations in only one page! (But, then the story would have been too short...)

Evidence that it works:

In a meta-analysis of two outcome studies, patients using hypnosis lost almost twice the weight of patients who did not receive hypnosis during treatment for weight loss. Kirsch, Irving (1996). Hypnotic enhancement of cognitive-behavioral weight loss treatments--Another meta-reanalysis. Journal of Consulting and Clinical Psychology.

A study on the treatment of obesity (Bolocofsky and Coulthard-Morris. 1985) showed a superiority of the combination of behavioral therapy and hypnosis even with a catamnesis of 24 month.

Hypnosis alters habitual behaviors such as snacking, lowers or removes cravings, creates motivation to exercise and can change beliefs in such a way that healthy foods become more enjoyable than fatty foods.

Weight loss hypnosis also works because it changes pre-suppositions. A pre-supposition for many overweight people is 'I'm going to eat all the food on my plate, because I don't want to waste it.' Hypnotherapy is good for drawing on knowledge that you already have. Most people do know the difference between healthy and unhealthy foods, and hypnosis can motivate them to put this knowledge into practice.

Cautions:

Clients who come to hypnosis - or begin any weight loss program - often have "magical thoughts" about results. Realistic expectations and goals should be discussed, and healthy levels of weight loss should be the target.

Healthy weight loss is gradual. It would be unhealthy for a client to lose 25 pounds in the next two weeks, if not impossible. We want our clients to experience weight loss in a realistic and beneficial way. We do not want our clients to develop eating disorders or aversions to food.

Losing one to two pounds a week for women and two to three pounds for men is realistic, attainable, and healthy. If our client wants to lose 20 pounds and it takes them eight to ten weeks, I think that is probably appropriate. We need to educate our client that hypnosis will work for them, but it will take time. The two things together, time and new associations are a combination that leads to success.

The client must understand that hypnosis is not some magic wand that we wave and their extra pounds vanish; hypnosis works to get their subconscious mind on track, so that they are better able to commit to putting their energy and effort into the program. The only way to lose weight is to consume fewer calories than the body burns in a day. This means that the hypnosis client, just like anyone else, must adjust their food intake (quality and quantity) and increase their physical exercise in order for the change to be successful. Hypnosis helps the client's internal motivations for following through with these necessary steps.

I think we need to become knowledgeable about the diagnosis of eating disorders that some clients who come to us for treatment of weight loss may have. We may discover during the assessment interview that a client is using a bunch of other unhealthy methods to try and lose weight, from pills to starvation diets, and having knowledge of those things is really essential.

Habit Control

Hypnosis is also effective for general habit control, and especially those habits that derive from nervous type conditions. After all, habits are controlled by the unconscious mind, and hypnosis is great for aiding relaxation and reducing anxiety.

Cigarette smoking is more than a habit; it is also nicotine addiction. Habits are things like nail biting, hair chewing, knuckle cracking, throat noises, coughing, tics, and so forth. Habits differ from addiction because there is not a physiological dependency on the behavior. Withdrawal from habits is only emotional, rather than physical (although some habits may require physical healing). Habits are usually products of subconscious associations and learning patterns, although personality characteristic may come into play, including perhaps obsessive traits and poor anxiety management skills.

Several research studies have found that hypnotherapy is effective with pediatric patients who experienced habitual tic disorders, habitual coughs, and even breathing difficulties. However, sometimes deep-seeded psychological impulses may require multiple sessions because the habit is so deeply ingrained.

Hypnotherapy for changing or eliminating habits often requires multiple sessions and the targeted development of alternative behaviors.

Alcoholism and Drug Addiction

The official position of some professional organizations is that alcohol and drug addiction should not be treated with hypnosis.

Personally, I think the opposite is true. I spent over ten years working as a drug and alcohol counselor in traditional 12-Step oriented treatment centers, and I cannot think of anything more effective for managing the physical symptoms of withdrawal distress than self-hypnosis. Hypnosis is easily incorporated with other modalities of drug and alcohol treatment, from AA programs to cognitive-behavioral therapy programs.

Addictions and habits are the domain of the unconscious mind, and the unconscious mind is the domain of the hypnotist, and therefore hypnosis is very effective for dealing with addictions and habits of all sorts.

However, we must recognize that there may be a need for medically supervised detox. Detoxification from alcohol and drugs can be complex, and it can put a person's life at risk. Therefore, if you do see a client for help recovering from addiction there should definitely be a physician referral so the client can be evaluated for any physical complications that may arise from withdrawal.

Evidence that it works:

Am J Clin Hypn. 2004 Apr;46(4):281-97

In a research study on self-hypnosis for relapse prevention training with chronic drug/alcohol users, individuals who played self-hypnosis audiotapes "at least 3 to 5 times a week," at 7-week follow-up, reported the highest levels of self-esteem and serenity, and the least anger/impulsivity, in comparison to the minimal-practice and control groups.

Emotional and Psychiatric Disorders

If you are a licensed mental health professional providing hypnotherapy in the context of emotional and psychiatric disorders, you should experience no difficulty from a liability or professional ethics perspective. However, if you are not licensed as a mental health professional it is important to recognize the limitations of your training. Psychiatric illnesses are the domain of the licensed professional, and so if you feel that an issue is out of your league please immediately refer the client.

Now, this does not mean that the hypnotist cannot help someone who is depressed. Depression is a normal human experience. However, when it becomes a catastrophic illness such as with suicidal ideation or bipolar disorder and other complex psychiatric issues, then it's time for a referral.

Dealing with general depression or anxiety or fears related to phobias is certainly in the context of hypnotism apart from professional therapy, but take these cautions to heart. Building a referral network and working with professional peers to determine what is and what is not within the domain of work that you do can save the non-licensed hypnotist a lot of time and grief.

There are four areas commonly associated with hypnotherapy related to emotional and psychiatric disorders:

- **Generalized Anxiety and Panic Disorders**
- **Post-Traumatic Stress Disorder**
- **Phobias**
- **Depression**

Generalized Anxiety and Panic Disorders

If you open up the DSM-IV (the APA's *Diagnostic and Statical Manual of Mental Disorders, Volume 4*), you will see that the first eight criteria for the diagnosis of panic disorder are all physical; heart palpitation, sweatiness, trembling etc. Panic and anxiety are very physical emotions and our bodies respond strongly. Learning to take physical control over emotions is something that hypnotherapy is particularly good at teaching. Many studies have shown significant reduction in anxiety and panic levels by people treated with hypnotherapy, extending as far out as three months post-therapy.

Hypnosis, with an emphasis on teaching physical skills for managing anxiety, can help clients in a number of ways: it can reprogram the subconscious to automatically use healthy coping strategies, teach a client how to calm themselves down physically, and help a person dissociate from unrealistic fears.

Evidence that it works:

Three-year follow-up and clinical implications of a mindfulness meditation-based stress reduction intervention in the treatment of anxiety disorders.

John J. Miller M.D., Ken Fletcher Ph.D., and Jon Kabat-Zinn Ph.D. - Department of Psychiatry, University of Massachusetts Medical Center, Worcester, Massachusetts, USA

The Stress Reduction Clinic, Department of Medicine, Division of Preventive and Behavioral Medicine, University of Massachusetts Medical Center, Worcester, Massachusetts, USA

Abstract:

A previous study of 22 medical patients with DSM-III-R-defined anxiety disorders showed clinically and statistically significant improvements in subjective and objective symptoms of anxiety and panic following an 8-week outpatient physician-referred group stress reduction intervention based on mindfulness meditation. Twenty subjects demonstrated significant reductions in Hamilton and Beck Anxiety and Depression scores post-intervention and at 3-month follow-up.

<u>*Cautions:*</u>

Anxiety is a natural emotion, and just like depression and anger, it can produce both positive and negative results. Getting rid of all anxiety or all fears is not necessarily a good thing. Anxiety can serve as a warning instrument for self-protection. In this context, clients should carefully evaluate their anxiety and discover what it is telling them.

Post-Traumatic Stress Disorder

Hypnosis is effective for post-traumatic stress disorder because it helps replace disturbing imagery, as we discussed earlier when I shared my car wreck experience. Combining the principles of NLP with hypnosis can be quite effective for specific phobias and PTSD. The caution with PTSD is, of course, the risk for abreaction, which we also discussed earlier, and it is something we need to be prepared for if we are treating post-traumatic stress disorder.

<u>*Evidence that it works:*</u>

Travel Phobias

By Iain B. McIntosh[1]

Journal of Travel Medicine, Volume 2 Page 99 - June 1995

doi:10.1111/j.1708-8305.1995.tb00635.x

"Hypnotherapy can be very successful, especially in people who present within a few days of impending flight. Hypnotherapy incorporates trance induction, ego-strengthening, relaxation, desensitization, and autohypnosis in a therapeutic program."

New uses of hypnosis in the treatment of post-traumatic stress disorder.

by Spiegel D, Cardena E.

Department of Psychiatry and Behavioral Sciences, Stanford University School of Medicine.
J Clin Psychiatry. 1990 Oct;51 Suppl:39-43; discussion 44-6.

Hypnosis is associated with the treatment of post-traumatic stress disorder (PTSD) for two reasons: (1) the similarity between hypnotic phenomena and the symptoms of PTSD, and (2) the utility of hypnosis as a tool in treatment. Physical trauma produces a sudden discontinuity in cognitive and emotional experience that often persists after the trauma is over. This results in symptoms such as psychogenic amnesia, intrusive reliving of the event as if it were recurring, numbing of responsiveness, and hyper-sensitivity to stimuli.

Two studies have shown that Vietnam veterans with PTSD have higher than normal hypnotizability scores on standardized tests. Likewise, a history of physical abuse in childhood has been shown to be strongly associated with dissociative symptoms later in life. Furthermore, dissociative symptoms during and soon after traumatic experience predict later PTSD. Formal hypnotic procedures are especially helpful because this population is highly hypnotizable. Hypnosis provides controlled access to memories that may otherwise be kept out of consciousness.

New uses of hypnosis in the psychotherapy of PTSD victims involve coupling access to the dissociated traumatic memories with positive restructuring of those memories. Hypnosis can be used to help patients face and bear a traumatic experience by embedding it in a new context, acknowledging helplessness during the event, and yet linking that experience with remoralizing memories such as efforts at self-protection, shared affection with friends who were killed, or the ability to control the environment at other times. In this way, hypnosis can be used to provide controlled access to memories that are then placed into a broader perspective. Patients can be taught self-hypnosis techniques that allow them to work through traumatic memories and thereby reduce spontaneous unbidden intrusive recollections.

The Additive Benefit of Hypnosis and Cognitive-Behavioral Therapy in Treating Acute Stress Disorder.

By Bryant, Richard A.; Moulds, Michelle L.; Guthrie, Rachel M.; Nixon, Reginald D. V.

Journal of Consulting and Clinical Psychology. 73(2), Apr 2005, 334-340

This research represents the first controlled treatment study of hypnosis and cognitive- behavioral therapy (CBT) of acute stress disorder (ASD). Civilian trauma survivors (N 87) who met criteria for ASD were randomly allocated to 6 sessions of CBT, CBT combined with hypnosis (CBT-hypnosis), or supportive counseling (SC). CBT comprised exposure, cognitive restructuring, and anxiety management.

CBT-hypnosis comprised the CBT components with each imaginal exposure preceded by a hypnotic induction and suggestions to engage fully in the exposure. In terms of treatment completers (n 69), fewer participants in the CBT and CBT-hypnosis groups met criteria for posttraumatic stress disorder at post treatment and 6-month follow-up than those in the SC group. CBT-hypnosis resulted in greater reduction in re-experiencing symptoms at post treatment than CBT. These findings suggest that hypnosis may have use in facilitating the treatment effects of CBT for posttraumatic stress.

Cautions:

Clients who define themselves by their traumas or a victim role need to redefine a new identity in order to actually make healthy, positive changes.

Complex PTSD can be a catastrophic psychiatric illness, its complexity going beyond hypnotherapy as a sole intervention in many cases, necessitating referral to a qualified mental health professional (who practices solution-focused therapy) for long-term treatment.

Phobias

Fear of flying can stem from prior events, such as an emergency landing, or becoming ill on a plane as a child, or from a generalized anxiety, or a specific fear such as mechanical failure or terrorism. Fear of flying can also originate as another anxiety disorder, such as a generalized anxiety that becomes more severe in the controlled situation of an aircraft, or as a manifestation of claustrophobia. Fear of flying occurs more frequently now than in the past, and it can debilitate individuals, leading to erratic behavior on flights with legal consequences, or derail certain career paths, and it can keep people from enjoying all that life has to offer including friends and family.

Specific phobias also include reptiles, insects, mice, clowns, or other specific fears that manifest in an otherwise healthy person's life. The fear can actually be of just about anything, and phobias to one degree or another are common in the general population.

Regression therapy strategies, such as the Fast Phobia Cure (you can find information about this technique online), are often used by hypnotherapists when clients can isolate a specific actuating event that triggered the fear. In this case, going back and re-living the event from a different perspective (as a witness on the sidelines) can help desensitize a person, much like the neuro-lingustic strategy of visualization that allows a person to begin seeing themselves observing life difficulties (rather than participating directly) in an effort to reduce the importance of the actuating event.

Phobias, such as fear of flying, fear of snakes spiders or heights or closed spaces may prevent the client from living a normal life. Hypnotherapy is great for addressing specific phobias because it creates new physical and psychological responses, which allow them to eliminate the old strategy or pattern of thinking that used to cause them fear.

Phobias are often an example of 'one time learning.' Someone is attacked by a dog as a child, and is from then on petrified of any and all dogs. When they see even the tiniest puppy, they create mental imagery of them being attacked and mauled. When we replace this negative mental imagery with more calming and positive thought patterns and reduce the impact of the fear response, phobias can be eliminated.

Depression

Michael Yapko, in his landmark book that we previously mentioned, *Treating Depression with Hypnosis*, comes down hard on the psychiatric and pharmaceutical industries who have sold the lie to Americans that depression is as simple as a chemical imbalance that can be "rebalanced" with anti-depressants.

Yapko does concede that biology can play a role in depression, but points to the fact that most depressions are holistic in nature. His tome makes a point that I have often made: we are much more than the sum total of our dopamine and serotonin receptors; our experiences in life go far beyond brain chemistry.

Those who view medication as a first line treatment for depression are simplistic in their understanding of the human condition. In the past, hypnosis was viewed as contraindicated for patients who were depressed. However, new research suggests that not only can hypnosis be utilized with the depressed person; it can also be highly effective.

Hypnosis draws on client strengths and existing coping strategies. It amplifies positive attributes that individuals already possess, to help them solve problems - and these are the characteristics of successful treatment protocols for depression.

It is true that biology can play a role in why some people are depressed, and anti-depressants can help some people function better - but they are less effective than regular exercise and traditional cognitive-behavioral approaches to treating depression. I believe that you can only function as well emotionally as you are fit physically. Hypnotherapy can be used to simultaneously impact our physical, emotional and spiritual health.

Of course, the primary caution with depression is suicidal ideation. If you are going to treat depressed individuals it is essential that you have some resources for assessments of suicidal ideation, and if you feel your client is suicidal, please strongly consider referral to a qualified professional.

A great resource for any level of professional, whether you are licensed or not, is the ASIQ; the Adult Suicidal Ideation Questionnaire. It is available from PAR, Psychological Assessment Resources Company. There are several depression and suicidal ideation tools on the market which you may want to research if you see depressed clients, but I personally like the ASIQ because it yields not only the score for the level of suicidal ideation, but it also highlights critical indicators.

Hypnosis can make people feel good. It can give them new perspectives on life, allow them to see the positive side and to reframe things in a productive way. It is crucial however that for more serious clients we keep in mind the deeper potential psychological causes that may be behind the depression they are experiencing, and consider referral.

Pain Management

Hypnotherapy has great efficacy for treating pain, and it is all natural, unlike medications, which means no negative side effects. Our body responds to our mind, and pain is a mental thing. 'What the mind can conceive, the body can achieve' is a statement frequently heard in hypnotherapy, and it is absolutely true.

Research studies have demonstrated the efficacy of clinical hypnosis for pain management in virtually every single medical setting, from treatment for headaches and migraines, arthritis, child birth, bone, muscle and joint pain, surgical anesthesia and post-surgical recovery, and severe burns. The caution is that sometimes hypnotherapists have the belief that if you are using hypnosis, there is no need for adjunct pain management medication. There has to be a balance, and it should come from the client in conjunction with their medical doctor.

Hypnosis may help some clients to avoid high levels of medications, so they can function cognitively, intellectually, and spiritually at a higher level. There is a difference between giving someone ten oxycontin a day for a headache, and giving morphine to the dying cancer patient. Balance and common sense. In many cases, hypnotherapy is best used as an adjunct treatment rather than a replacement treatment, however in other cases the client may be able to avoid pain medication and its side effects all together. Encourage your clients to use hypnotherapy consistent with their goals and what is medically appropriate.

<u>*Evidence that it works:*</u>

Hypnosis and Pain Reduction: The Latest Research

University of Iowa News Release
March 14, 2005

Brain Imaging Studies Investigate Pain Reduction By Hypnosis

Although hypnosis has been shown to reduce pain perception, it is not clear how the technique works. Identifying a sound, scientific explanation for hypnosis' effect might increase acceptance and use of this safe pain-reduction option in clinical settings.

Researchers at the University of Iowa Roy J. and Lucille A. Carver College of Medicine and the Technical University of Aachen, Germany, used functional magnetic resonance imaging (fMRI) to find out if hypnosis alters brain activity in a way that might explain pain reduction. The results are reported in the November-December 2004 issue of *Regional Anesthesia and Pain Medicine*.

The researchers found that volunteers under hypnosis experienced significant pain reduction in response to painful heat. They also had a distinctly different pattern of brain activity compared to when they were not hypnotized and experienced the painful heat. The changes in brain activity suggest that hypnosis somehow blocks the pain signal from getting to the parts of the brain that perceive pain.

"The major finding from our study, which used fMRI for the first time to investigate brain activity under hypnosis for pain suppression, is that we see reduced activity in areas of the pain network and increased activity in other areas of the brain under hypnosis," said Sebastian Schulz-Stubner, M.D., Ph.D., UI assistant professor (clinical) of anesthesia and first author of the study. "The increased activity might be specific for hypnosis or might be non-specific, but it definitely does something to reduce the pain signal input into the cortical structure."

... Hypnosis was successful in reducing pain perception for all 12 participants. Hypnotized volunteers reported either no pain or significantly reduced pain (less than 3 on the 0-10 pain scale) in response to the painful heat.

Under hypnosis, fMRI showed that brain activity was reduced in areas of the pain network, including the primary sensory cortex, which is responsible for pain perception.

Review of the Efficacy of Clinical Hypnosis with Headaches and Migraines

The International Journal of Clinical and Experimental Hypnosis; Volume 55, Number 2 - April 2000

The twelve-member National Institute of Health Technology Assessment Panel on Integration of Behavioral and Relaxation Approaches into the Treatment of Chronic Pain and Insomnia reviewed existing outcome studies on hypnosis with cancer pain. They concluded that research-based evidence suggests hypnosis to be effective with some chronic pain, including tension headaches. Their paper presents an updated review of existing literature on the efficacy of hypnosis for the treatment of headaches and migraines, and determines that it meets the clinical psychology research criteria for being a well-established and efficacious treatment, essentially free of the side effects, risks of adverse reactions, and ongoing expense associated with traditional medication treatments.

Cautions:

Pain is an important signal and it does serve a very important purpose. While pain is unpleasant, it is an indicator that something is wrong and should be recognized as such. Never use hypnosis for pain control unless you are sure it is 100% safe to do so.

Sexual Issues

The brain is the largest and most important sex organ in the body, and reprogramming the brain through hypnosis can help to alleviate or deal with unhealthy associations (perhaps fears or phobias from bad past experiences), failing physical responses (mental or physical origins), and other insecurities or issues related to sexual intimacy.

If you are going to work with individuals or couples to improve sexual dysfunction, it is important that you become comfortable and familiar with this topic from a professional standpoint. You cannot be a prude, and you must be able to discuss these private issues frankly, but from a clinical perspective. There are numerous resources available – hypnotist Wendi Friesen has some great material on the subject of intimacy – so do the research, and study it well.

And again, recognize that if you are not a licensed mental health professional, you may simply not be qualified to help with some issues. If a client's topic – symptoms, experiences – seem to be over your head or fall into a more pathological realm, please, please refer.

Once more: There is no shame in referral.

Stress Management

Let us now focus on the management of stress, which is quite a self-explanatory issue, as hypnosis and relaxation are very often combined. Hypnosis teaches relaxation through therapeutic breathing, muscle tension and relaxation, and the visual imagery necessary to experience deep peace. In short, it teaches people who don't know how to relax, how to purposefully, consciously relax both mind and body.

What are the cautions? Generally speaking, there are few cautions, other than perhaps to let clients engaged in PMR know that if they feel an isolated deep pain in any part of the body while doing the 'tension and relaxation' exercises, strength training at the gym might help, and consulting with a physician regarding usual pain can rule out bone and muscle injuries that have gone undiagnosed. Also, client conditions such as supposed stress-related headaches could possibly be indicative of other problems, and should be evaluated by a physician to rule out anything like a brain tumor.

Again, take the time to ask questions of your client in the interview assessment process. When do they feel stressed, what are the primary causes, what their symptoms are, what have they tried – what has worked and what has failed – and what they hope to achieve using hypnosis as it concerns stress management.

As a side note, not drinking alcohol, avoiding caffeine and other drugs - including nicotine - can help you to feel rested at night and to feel stress free. Although in the short run, these substances seem to produce relaxation, they physically affect the body in the opposite manner. Finding a natural way to depart from the stressors of the day is essential, and hypnosis can be a positive way to do this.

The more you know about your client's lifestyle, the better able you will be to develop targeted suggestions for lasting change.

Testing and Exam Anxiety

In general, the category of test anxiety falls under the heading of stress management, rather than emotional-related anxiety and panic problems. I know a hypnotist in Texas who lives in college town, and 90% of his practice is devoted to treating test anxiety related to students preparing for medical or law school entrance examinations, term exams, professional oral examinations, state boards, and so forth.

Hypnotherapy for test-taking works because it helps the person relax, and when they are more relaxed they are able to focus, which aids their short-term memory. Studies show that people engaging in hypnosis prior to taking examinations do better than those who do not.

The caution is that naturally some clients have magical thinking, like, "I'll go see a hypnotist and I'll be able to recall everything. I won't even need to study!" And then they bomb the test. The client should be instructed to study as normal. Hypnosis is not a substitute for learning material. We do not want to reinforce unrealistic expectations, so be careful in your marketing if you want to attract these kinds of clients. Instead, we want them to know that hypnotherapy works for managing anxiety and increasing relaxation. It provides a feeling of rest and well-being, and aids in memory and focus.

The hypnotic state is also a state of accelerated learning, which makes sense when you think about suggestion in terms of us teaching the client. If we teach our clients self-hypnosis skills to use in conjunction with their studies, they will have a lot more success with recall and understanding. Long-term memory is, after all, the domain of the unconscious.

<u>*Evidence that it works:*</u>

Psychosocial and immune effects of self-hypnosis training for stress management throughout the first semester of medical school

WG Whitehouse, DF Dinges, EC Orne, SE Keller, BL Bates, NK Bauer, P Morahan,
BA Haupt, MM Carlin, PB Bloom, L Zaugg and MT Orne
Institute of Pennsylvania Hospital, University of Pennsylvania Medical School, Philadelphia, USA.

This study was a 19-week prospective conducted to determine the effectiveness of a self-hypnosis/relaxation intervention to relieve symptoms of psychological distress and moderate immune system reactivity to examination stress in 35 first-year medical students. Twenty-one subjects were randomly selected for training in the use of self-hypnosis as a coping skill and were encouraged to practice regularly and to maintain daily diary records related to mood, sleep, physical symptoms, and frequency of relaxation practice. An additional 14 subjects received no explicit training in stress-reduction strategies, but completed similar daily diaries. Self-report psychosocial and symptom measures, as well as blood draws, were obtained at four time points: orientation, late semester, examination period, and post semester recovery.

It was found that significant increases in stress and fatigue occurred during the examination period, paralleled by increases in counts of B lymphocytes and activated T lymphocytes, PHA-induced and PWM-induced blasto-genesis, and natural killer cell (NK) cytotoxicity. No immune decreases were observed. Subjects in the self-hypnosis condition reported significantly less distress and anxiety than their nonintervention counterparts, but the two groups did not differ with respect to immune function. Nevertheless, within the self-hypnosis group, the quality of the exercises (i.e. relaxation ratings) predicted both the number of NK cells and NK activity.

It was concluded that stress associated with academic demands affects immune function, but immune suppression is not inevitable. Practice of self-hypnosis reduces distress, without differential immune effects. However, individual responses to the self-hypnosis intervention appear to predict immune outcomes.

Bettering the Good

In addition to alleviating problems, hypnosis can also be used to make the good things better. This is called generative improvement.

Not all stress is 'bad.' Like the emotion anger, stress can often be a positive motivator and energizer. The difference is in perception, and controlling and channeling the stress to make it work for you in these healthy ways.

Hypnosis can be used to target the use of natural stress for focus, to enhance and unleash physical and mental resources, allowing them to become better at sports, to fuel creativity and enhance confidence, to improve academic performance, solidify personal relationships, and deepen general happiness, health, and wellbeing.

–

An educational and skills discussion on the issues above could fill an entire book, each. In this text, we have provided a brief overview and it is now up to you to further research and study the areas which interest you most, or have most relevance for the clients on your caseload.

Remember, every client is different – different experiences, expectations, education, spiritual needs, physical conditions, and ultimate goals. Take the time in your interview assessment session to get to know your client a little, listen to what they say, ask questions to clarify, and do your best to develop suggestive therapy plan to help them achieve lasting positive changes.

CHAPTER 12

Ethics, Morality and Legal Principles Related to Hypnotherapy

There are certain ethical requirements and guidelines that you need to adhere to in order to make sure the work you do is not only ethical, but also falls within the legislative constraints of wherever you happen to be living.

Hypnotherapy is primarily an unregulated profession. Unlike other licenseable professions such as marriage and family therapy, social working or psychology, in most states just about anyone can hang out a shingle and say, "Hi, I'm Jack/Jane Smith, a certified hypnotist." Some states do have constraints regarding who may advertise, how they may advertise, and the types of services that they may deliver, but only a few actually license or register hypnotists. However, the ethical considerations, whether you live in a state that regulates hypnosis or does not, need to be addressed.

It is my opinion that the profession of hypnotherapy will move forward when responsible professional associations take it upon themselves to provide ethical guidelines to their members and those members adhere strictly to the ethical guidelines. When we have professionals practicing outside the boundaries of professional associations and their specific codes of ethics, we usually run into difficulties with the perception of hypnotherapy as a professional practice.

I hope in this chapter to not only answer some questions, but really set the foundation for you in regards to practicing hypnotherapy responsibly and within the guidelines of what is generally considered by the professional associations of today to be good practice.

The Code of Ethics that we'll use in this text comes from the ICBCH, the International Certification Board for Clinical Hypnotherapy, because I find it particularly comprehensive. There are other professional associations with codes of ethics, but upon review, I think that the others are not quite as specific as the ICBCH 's. Of course those whose members are strictly licensed mental health professionals probably assume that their members are already operating under the ethical codes of their respective profession, and perhaps that explains their vagueness.

Let us take a look at the issues that are most important to us regarding the moral and ethical practice of clinical hypnosis, and hopefully this brief discussion will clarify some questions and provide some guidance.

Morality

First, let us examine five moral principles that should guide any professional's actions and decision-making processes, whether you are a massage therapist, a hypnotist, a marriage family therapist or a psychologist.

Five Moral Principles
- for Providing Ethical Care

Autonomy

In all of the actions we take as hypnotherapists, our goal is to help our clients function independently. Years ago, I was one of the few licensed mental health professionals in a very, very small town in Texas. Another psychotherapist in town retired and referred all of her clients to me. One day I received a call from a client who "had to see me right away." I did not have a chance to look at the case notes ahead of the time, but I said to come on over.

She arrived and during introductions I glanced at her case history and saw that she had been with the previous therapist for about two years, so the first question I asked was, "I see you've been in therapy for the last two years. What you have been working on?" She said, "Detachment." I thought that was pretty darn amusing, and so I asked, "Who is it that you are trying to detach from?" She said, "Oh! I am trying to detach from my grandmother." She looked about thirty-five, and I thought it was little odd that the therapeutic issue consuming her for two years was how to detach from grandma.

Despite my bemusement I was curious, and I had a job to do, so I asked her to describe her Grandmother. According to her, Grandma was a horrible person who had dominated and affected much of her life. I found myself empathizing with the client and thinking, 'If I had a Grandma like that, I too would want to be as detached as possible!'

Then the reality-therapist in me kicked in. "Hey, quick question here. You are thirty-five years old. Why don't you move out of your grandmother's house?" She looked at me strangely and said, "I don't live with my grandmother."

I paused, then asked, "Where does your grandmother live?" She said, "Washington." I stared at her with a look of befuddlement and asked, "Your grandmother lives in Washington? You have spent two years in therapy in Texas, learning how to detach from your grandmother who lives in Washington?" She nodded and offered a sheepish grin. I said, "Your therapeutic assignment is not to come to therapy any longer. You need to find a real friend, one you don't have to pay to talk to every single week."

You see, the prior therapist had become her best friend, instead of helping her to find a best friend. We can give clients advice and it may even be from our own experiences, but we cannot be their 12-Step sponsor. We can have unconditional positive regard for our clients and accept them, but we cannot be their mother. We can actually genuinely like our clients, but it is not our job to be their friend. Our job is to be a paid temporary professional who helps them to find a real friend, a real mother, a real sponsor, and real situational supports that help them solve problems.

When a client comes in to our office, our first goal should be to help them function independently. This is, by the way, one of the reasons why I like hypnotherapy, as it is by nature a brief form of therapy, a quick intervention. Certainly there are complex cases that may require multiple sessions. For example, the standard recommended treatment protocol for irritable bowel syndrome is seven sessions, and substantial weight loss treatment often follows a multi-session protocol over several months. However, most cases, from smoking cessation to phobia treatment, generally require only one to three sessions, max.

Hypnotherapy promotes autonomy so our client can function apart from a therapeutic relationship. The goal of a good therapist is to get rid of their clients, not to fill another billable hour.

Beneficence

The basic concept of beneficence is the help we provide should be beneficial to the client. Our clients come to us for help with specific problems, and it is our job to help them find beneficial solutions. Reading a one-size-fits-all script may help a little, but probably would not be near as beneficial as taking the time to construct individual therapeutic suggestions targeted to utilize the client's specific strengths and resources to meet their individual needs.

Furthermore, we need to give our clients what they want and ask for, not create more reasons to see them more frequently. Providing unnecessary sessions is not beneficial.

Non malfeasance

Not only should we promote goodness through beneficial outcomes, but we also want to avoid doing harm to our clients.

First and foremost on this list, of course, is to never, ever have any kind of romantic or sexual relations with anyone who is or ever has been your client. Never. Period. This sets up an unequal, unhealthy and unethical dynamic. Don't do it.

We can do harm to our clients by revealing confidential information. There is no need to ever discuss your clients' cases with anyone outside of a professional setting. Yes, you may discuss issues with other hypnotists, therapists or doctors for purposes of guidance or referral, but you should not chat up your friends at a party about Mr. Smith, whom you saw for sexual dysfunction last week.

We can do harm to our clients by being incompetent. If you are unsure about a condition or treatment approach, get educated or refer. Do not waste your client's time or money, or take the risk of doing harm by being arrogant.

Do not make your clients believe that you have powers that you do not have. Be open and honest about the hypnotic process, how it works and what they should expect, from the session itself to the end results.

We avoid doing harm by providing professional, ethical, quality care.

Justice

Justice requires that we provide equal treatment to all people. It is okay to have religious beliefs and biases. This is America and you are allowed to believe anything you want about anything. However, while we will always bring our values into the counseling process with us, we have an obligation to provide just services. In order to be a competent professional, we must put our own moral judgments, biases, and beliefs aside, so that we can provide equal treatment to all people.

As a hypnotherapist, you will meet all kinds of clients, including many who don't share the same morals, foundations, and beliefs as you. If you are unable to provide equal treatment to all clients, then you need to find a different environment to work in.

Fidelity

It is important to keep our promises. Fidelity implies being truthful and loyal, and being worthy of that trust. Our clients look to us as a model. As I mentioned previously, modeling healthy behavior by not smoking, not being a drunk, not overeating, but being a model for health and fitness is really essential for a hypnotist who promotes health-related services.

Likewise, we also need to model for our clients fidelity by being on time for sessions. When we say we will follow through on something, we follow through - by calling back, by being available and accessible to our clients. Fidelity is essential for providing good care.

In reality, ethics and morality are largely a matter of common sense. Provided you have the right intentions and think through your professional actions, you should find remaining ethical a simple task.

Five Hallmarks of Good Therapy
– for Reducing Liability

Yes, there are many more than five, but these five strike me as particularly crucial for the work we do, not only to be a good hypnotist in general, but to also help minimize your liability.

Our clients come to us because they want us to provide good services; they expect that we will help them make changes and do so effectively. When we provide good care and competent services we are doing our jobs well, and we are also safe on the legal front.

Please understand that I cannot tell you how to not get sued. There is an ambulance-chasing trial attorney on every corner who, for a $45 filing fee, will come after you for anything. However, I can tell you that if you are sued in civil court, the best defense is to simply have done your job properly and have acted competently and professionally at every stage of the way.

Good Hypnotherapy has Measurable Success

I believe success should be measured by actual recordable change, rather than merely by emotions observed. Change means whether the presenting problem is actually fixed, or not.

Often we don't feel like we have an objective way of measuring success. We may say, well, if the client leaves happy then we have done our job. Well, if the client's objective when they came to you was to leave your office happy in general, then I suppose so, but what about the issues you addressed during the session? Emotion seems both for us and for clients to be a simple way to measure success, but that is just a temporary illusion. It does not matter if they are happy when they leave if they begin smoking again three hours later. We measure success by helping the client achieve real goals.

Good Hypnotherapy Focuses on the Present and the Future, Rather than Dwelling on the Past

The key word here is dwelling. The past is important. Our experiences do shape us, influence us, and lead us to where we are today. Sometimes the culmination of life experiences can be extremely difficult, bringing clients to the point where therapeutic services are desired, so it is essential to understand our client's framework in the context of their past, so that we may help them make changes for the future.

However, often our clients often would rather talk about the past, because that is lot easier than taking responsibility now for action in the future, and some therapists like talking about the past, because it fills billable hours. Good therapy, however, does not focus on or dwell on the past. It recognizes its importance, but focuses on the present and the future and asks the question: What are the tasks that need done to move from the present scene to the preferred scene?

Our goal is not to change the past, which is a good thing since that cannot be done. Our goal as a hypnotist is to help our clients make changes so as not to repeat the past, to move forward towards a positive, desired goal.

Good Hypnotherapy Unlocks our Client's Strengths

A lot of individuals have a lot of problems, but they also have unique strengths. I may not be able to completely fix what is wrong, but I can take the strengths that exist in that individual's life and use them to compensate for their deficits, so they can choose a healthy manner of living for the future.

When I work with clients to find out ways to help them quit smoking, one of the things I may ask is, "Okay, you have been smoking for the last ten years. Were there any circumstances in the last ten years where you normally would have smoked, but you did not?" Maybe they spent weekends with their mother who still doesn't know they smoke. Or maybe they smoke every day except sometimes Sundays, because they go to church. I want to draw from my client's existing repertoire of resources and personality strengths to help them solve problems.

Good Hypnotherapy Mobilizes Friends and Family into Active Support

For a lot of issues, people need other people in their everyday lives to help them stay focused and maintain positive change. When working with the individual losing weight, I want to try to find solid situational supports, the people who will help them maintain healthy food choices and support their exercise goals. A lot of times losing weight is a struggle because those they share the refrigerator with haven not decided to make the same healthy choices. We want the client to identify friends, family and coworkers who can help reinforce positive change.

Good Hypnotherapy Teaches Skills

Hypnosis clients learn how to relax, how to align their conscious and unconscious resources, how to go into productive trance states and manage stress, and how to truly be all that they can be, and this is good. Again, it is one thing for the client to be happy in our office, but we must provide them with the tools and skills they need to succeed at their goals once they leave our building.

Good suggestions teach the client how to draw upon their strengths, how to utilize support systems, and how to think and react differently to situations in positive, healthy ways.

Professional Ethics

As we begin to wind down, I want to go over the relevant ethical guidelines provided by the International Certification Board for Clinical Hypnotherapy in detail. As mentioned before, I have chosen to use the ICBCH's code because I think it is more comprehensive than others.

When you look at professional organizations to join, become affiliated with, and/or to become certified by, take some time and see what these organizations have to offer. Those that do not have a Code of Ethics are probably not professional associations acting in the best interest of the members it certifies.

Please recognize also that while this Code refers to "Certified Hypnotherapists," the same concepts apply to "Certified Hypnotists" and even stage performers, as well.

ICBCH certified professionals adhere to the following Ethical Principles:

a.) ICBCH Certified Hypnotherapists promote client autonomy.

b.) ICBCH Certified Hypnotherapists respect clients and promote what is healthy for clients.

c.) ICBCH Certified Hypnotherapists do not engage in behaviors that cause harm to clients or that exploit clients.

d.) ICBCH Certified Hypnotherapists value continuing education and seek opportunities to continue to grow in knowledge.

e.) ICBCH Certified Hypnotherapists recognize both the benefits and the limitations of clinical hypnosis.

f.) ICBCH Certified Hypnotherapists promote hypnotherapy with demonstrated efficacy rather than pseudoscience or modalities of hypnosis that are merely speculative.

g.) ICBCH Certified Hypnotherapists accurately represent their educational experiences to clients.

h.) ICBCH Certified Hypnotherapists recognize the need for psychological and medical referrals to other professionals and build relationships with other disciplines of helping.

I.) ICBCH Certified Hypnotherapists provide clients with informed consent at the outset of hypnotherapy.

j.) ICBCH Certified Hypnotherapists keep client information confidential, except when required by law, or with the client's written consent prior to release of confidential information.

k.) ICBCH Certified Hypnotherapists avoid dual-relationships and sexual contact with clients.

l.) ICBCH Certified Hypnotherapists provide services in the context of professional business arrangements, and establish fees and payment arrangements clearly understood by clients.

m.) ICBCH Certified Hypnotherapists recognize the need to adhere to the principles of respecting others when publicly demonstrating hypnosis in non-clinical settings.

n.) ICBCH Certified Hypnotherapists accurately represent credentials.

o.) ICBCH Certified Hypnotherapists promote public awareness of hypnotherapy.

p) ICBCH Members do not solicit other members or clients about joining multi-level marketing programs.

Certified hypnotherapists promote autonomy. As you can see, the first few ideas are based on the moral principles we discussed a little while ago. Our goal is to help our clients function apart from the professional relationship and out in the real world.

Certified hypnotherapists respect their clients and promote what is healthy for clients. The number one reason why clients bring civil suits against professionals is not because they want the big bucks; they are motivated by anger, because they feel like they have been disrespected.

Certified hypnotherapists do not engage in behaviors that cause harm to or exploit clients. I have had the opportunity to do hypnosis with stars from Las Vegas, Hollywood and Broadway, and have had my picture taken with many, but never have I put the pictures or even their names up on my website. Never have I asked them to do personal testimonials, even though their endorsements would probably be good for my sales. It would be an exploitation of those clients to reveal their names. It is important for us to respect our clients and not use them for our own gain, whether they are famous or not.

As a hypnotist, it is important that you are constantly learning. A lot of people in professional therapy try to do only the minimum amount of continuing education required by the state each year, and I suppose that is their prerogative. However, in my opinion, it is essential for your own growth as a professional and for the good of your clients that you passionately immerse yourself in all the training and materials that you can find and practice your skills as much as possible, whether you are required to by your licensing or certifying associations, or not.

Once upon a time, I was treating an autistic client for another presenting problem. In that particular case, I remember looking at the records, seeing autism in the client history, and realizing that most everything I knew about autism I had learned from the movie *Rain Man*.

Even though I was a licensed mental health professional, I did not know much about autism or other childhood pervasive mental illness or psychiatric disorders. Even though I generally do not treat children, I started going to training workshops and bought books on this subject, so I would be able to increase my base of knowledge, so that I could better understand the history of some of the clients that I was seeing for adult chemical dependency counseling and adult traditional psychotherapy, as well as hypnotherapy.

Now, you may not be a licensed mental health professional, and you may not ever see many clients for issues beyond smoking cessation or weight loss, but it will be helpful to you – and your clients – if you study the available resources for many commonly seen illnesses and conditions. Continuing education, whether legally required or not, is another hallmark of good therapy, as you never know when you may need it.

Certified hypnotherapists recognize both the benefits and limitations of clinical hypnosis. Go to **scholar.google.com** - Google's scholarly journal search engine - and type in hypnotism and any disorder you can think of, and the results will probably surprise you. The evidence for the efficacy of hypnotherapy as a treatment modality with physical conditions, psychiatric conditions, and behavioral conditions is incredible, demonstrated time after time in journal articles for weight loss, smoking cessation, pain management, even management of allergy related symptoms, child birth, and more.

At the same time, while hypnotherapy is highly effective for many issues, there are also limitations. Some problems may require not only hypnotherapy, but traditional cognitive-behavioral or other forms of psychotherapy or medical treatment as well, in order to fully assist the client with making the long-term changes they need or desire. While hypnosis is remarkably effective, it is a matter of professional ethics that you realize it is not a magic solution to every problem.

Certified hypnotherapists promote hypnotherapy with a demonstrated efficacy, rather than speculative pseudo-science. Hypnotherapy, like assessment tools that are self-reports, is limited by the participant's willingness to engage in the process. We have to recognize the limitations. For example, memory is not like a video camera; hypnosis for memory recall, traumatic events, or forensics, can be inaccurate or embellished.

Certified hypnotherapists should also accurately represent their educational experiences to clients. The field of hypnotherapy is, of course, unregulated. As such, there are people who have no educational experience at all, not even a high school diploma, who are practicing clinical hypnosis. There is nothing wrong with that – other than I would call them a 'clinical hypnotist' and not a 'hypnotherapist' – however, I feel it is a matter of professional ethics that we do not overstate the education we have received.

Hypnosis itself is a learning process, and learning how to fully facilitate that process takes time. You must recognize that this text, as well as any other training or certification program, is an entry point, a starting point.

If you do not have a clinical degree and you read this book, you will know how to hypnotize somebody, but until you have hours and hours of practice and experience behind you, you will not be a competent hypnotherapist. It is important to represent ourselves accurately to clients, and at this early stage in your training, to represent yourself as a hypnotherapist would not be an ethical thing to do.

The certified hypnotherapist also recognizes the need for psychological and medical referrals to and from other professionals and builds relationships with other helping disciplines. Without a doubt, some of the clients on our caseload need to be referred for medical intervention. For example, an alcoholic client comes in and says, "I can't quit drinking. I struggled with this appointment since eight o'clock in the morning so that I could be sober for the first time and participate in this session." Great! I want them to be there, and I will provide services that can help them deal with the withdrawal symptoms they are experiencing the first day. However, I am also going to immediately refer them to a physician, because detoxification can be a dangerous process for some of our clients.

If a client comes to you because they want help during difficult periods like cancer treatment, post surgical procedures, or for other medical treatments, hypnosis can help them recover and manage their bodies. However, we need to refer them back for continued follow-up care necessary for their medical conditions, rather than simply letting them believe that because they feel good there's no need for aftercare or follow-up. In these cases, hypnosis should be viewed as a supplement to, rather than a replacement of, conventional medical treatment.

If we have clients with severe psychological or psychiatric disturbances, hypnosis can help them relax and take physical control over their emotions. It is okay to provide some hypnosis services to some individuals who have psychological or psychiatric difficulties. What is not okay is treating, without having a license, psychological and psychiatric difficulties. You will need to refer those individuals, as well.

Certified hypnotherapists provide clients with informed consent at the outset of therapy. We have discussed this before; informed consent educates clients about the process they will be engaging in. This occurs in the assessment intake and the pre-talk.

Certified hypnotherapists keep client information confidential, except when required by law, requested by a judge, or with the client's written consent prior to the release to family or referral sources. This is essential. Now, let me quickly address HIPAA Confidentiality. Most hypnotherapists do not practice in a HIPAA required environment. However, just so you are aware, the Health Insurance Portability Act regulations requires that certain federal security standards are met in regards to confidentiality of data transmitted electronically to third-party payers (insurance companies). Unless you are a licensed professional working with insurance companies, HIPAA is generally not something you will have to worry about, but taking extra precautions with your client's information is always a good thing.

Certified hypnotherapists need to avoid dual relationships and sexual contact with clients. Again, it is most likely a felony in the state where you live to have sex with anyone who has been or ever was a client. There are millions of other people who are not on your caseload, so please have sex with one of them. It really is that simple. There is absolutely no excuse for sexual conduct with a client. It is unacceptable. It is unprofessional. It always harms clients. It can never be justified in the context of competent clinical care.

Dual relationships – being friends with or doing business with a client outside the office - are difficult to manage and can be equally damaging to clients. They can put us in situations where false accusations can arise from hurt feelings and failure to respect the client. Liabilities and lawsuits come out of dual relationships. Having a referral network becomes essential in order to avoid a dual relationship.

Now, let's say I go to the same gas station every day to fill up my car, and one day the clerk says to me, "You know, I noticed that your credit card says Richard K. Nongard, and I think I've heard your name on radio ads. Do you do hypnosis?" I reply, "Yes, that's me, and I do." He then says, "Awesome, can you help my wife quit smoking?" I respond with, "Sure, here's my card." This situation is called networking; it is not a dual relationship. Refer your friends, neighbors, family and those you work with to someone else for hypnosis services.

Certified hypnotherapists provide services in the context of professional business arrangements and establish fees and payment arrangements clearly understood by clients. My payment arrangements are simple; cash, check, or charge. I suppose I would probably take gold bullion too, but no one has offered it. I don't barter. I don't exchange working on my car for hypnotherapy sessions.

Some clients like bartering, and it may appeal to us, but in the end, something about a barter relationship always feels unequal to one of the bartering parties. If you have something I want, I'm going to buy it from you. If I have something you want - hypnosis services - you are going to buy it from me, cash, check, or charge. This is really the only way to provide competent services.

Also, I let my clients know on the telephone when they schedule their first appointment that payments are expected at the time services are rendered. This information is also on my website.

Suppose I have a client that I am seeing for multiple sessions. Will I let them slide on payment for a session? Sure, they can catch me later or pay me next week. However, I will never carry a client for more than two sessions. Why? They will end up in debt owing me money, I will have to cut them off, and they will resent me when I go back and try to collect it from them, and we won't be making progress on their goals. It's just human nature.

I want my clients to pay me for the services I provide, and so my payment policies are clearly outlined in the orientation process. Will I provide services for free? Yes, to some people, some times. The profession has been good to me, and I think it is important for us to give back to the world around us. But, we need to be selective in picking the people who are most needy, who will benefit, and who will respect the gift we give them. To me, that is essential as well.

Certified hypnotherapists recognize the need to adhere to the principles of respecting others when publicly demonstrating hypnosis in non-clinical settings. Again, as you can tell by this text, I personally believe stage hypnosis is fine when the clients or subjects are respected. In my opinion, to say that a hypnotist should not be able to publicly demonstrate hypnosis for entertainment purposes is like saying that Hollywood should not be allowed to produce movies where people would experience anger or hurt or fear or sadness.

Certified Hypnotherapists accurately represent credentials. My business cards and stationary all say Richard K. Nongard, LMFT/CCH. This is because I am a state Licensed Marriage and Family Therapist, and I am a Certified Clinical Hypnotherapist.

Many non-licensed hypnotists will take courses and earn 'degrees' in hypnosis or hypnotherapy, and then call themselves a doctor. The truth is that there is not one fully accredited educational program in the United States that offers an actual degree in hypnosis or hypnotherapy, not a Bachelor's or Master's or Doctorate. The reason for this is that psychologists like to believe that hypnotherapy is their domain, alone. Whether their position is right or wrong is irrelevant to this discussion. In my experience, the average practicing non-licensed hypnotist generally has 100 times more education and knowledge of the field of clinical hypnosis than the average licensed psychologist ever received in graduate school.

The point is: Do not represent yourself to clients as having earned degrees or credentials that you have not. It is perfectly acceptable for you to take any course available on the planet in hypnosis, and I encourage you to take as many as possible, because the more training you have the better hypnotist you will be, and the better served your clients will be, as well. However, please take care not to get caught up in bogus credentials. Certification is one thing – it means you have taken a course, and hopefully passed some sort of comprehensive exam, and for this you have earned recognition through the form of a professional development certification credential, i.e. become a Certified Hypnotist. But certification is not the same as a degree, so please market yourself accordingly.

Certified Hypnotherapists should also promote public awareness of hypnotherapy. You should be on board for promoting public awareness and education about hypnosis, if for no other reason than to protect and further your own career.

Every year, legislation begins circulating in many states to restrict who can and cannot practice hypnotherapy and how it should be practiced. Some of those decisions, like the decision in Indiana that says 'group hypnosis' may have no more than three participants, are not really in the best interest of clients. Educating those who create legislation is important. Legislators only know what they know, and so they often vote the way someone tells them to vote. If no one offers an opposing ideal based on facts rather than protectionism, the bill may be passed and you may find yourself out of business.

The final ideal is that **ICBCH certified hypnotherapists do not solicit other members or clients about joining multi-level marketing programs.** The reason this statement exists is that many people are drawn to hypnosis because they are into non-traditional modalities for change in general, and that spectrum is quite broad. They may have learned about hypnosis from exposure to yoga or meditation, or they may have gone to a metaphysical fair and met a palm-reader or a past-life regressionist. No matter the origination, the fact is that many 'naturalists' or complementary and alternative medicine (CAM) proponents are also into multi-level marketing plans, from vitamins to hormones, pre-paid legal services and so forth. This is all fine, well and good, and I have no problem with that whatsoever – I have bought my own lifetime supply of miracle juice before – but clients are paying you for hypnosis services, not to have a chance at joining your down-line.

Can you offer supplements or trinkets in your office for clients to purchase if they so choose? Absolutely. Should you harass your clients about buying them or joining your program? Absolutely not. Let's say you are at a hypnosis convention. Should you call the hotel room of another hypnotist at six o'clock in the morning to tell them about a great opportunity you have to offer, as once happened to me? Most certainly not.

Quackery

A few final thoughts: I don't think we can talk about professional ethics and not talk about quacks. The field of mental health counseling is filled with quackery, and hypnosis is certainly not exempt. Personally, I think it is quackery when a client is depressed and goes to a physician to get a prescription for anti-depressants and is sent out the door without any other intervention being provided. We know that the most effective intervention is not medication but cardiovascular exercise three to four times a week. We know that if the doctor were to prescribe exercise and if the client were to follow through, then the client would benefit a lot more. This does not mean that I am opposed to medication, I just think we become quacks when we only do what is familiar to us without considering the alternatives. The one-size-fits-all treatment modality can become quackery, even when the intervention is valid.

Why is it that professionals become quacks? I have met some nice people who genuinely care about others, but whether in the field of medicine, chiropractic, hypnotherapy, or professional counseling, they crossed over into 'quackdom.' Why?

Boredom. They learn a new technique at a weekend seminar; maybe hypnosis, maybe EMDR, maybe nutritional consulting, and then they come back and apply it to every one of their clients on their caseload. A lot of people get excited about hypnosis, and then apply indiscriminately to everyone and all of the problems that they see without regard to the efficacy for some conditions, or even their client's desires.

Personal crisis. People often become quacks because they experience and then resolve a personal crisis. "I had a problem, and I got fixed this way, so this is the approach I am going to use with you. If you don't like my approach, go out there and have some more misery. Come back when you are ready to do it my way." In this example, I have become a quack because I have not even considered addressing my client's needs with any other set of skills that I can draw up on. Do not let your personal experiences, 'baggage' or bias obstruct the wellbeing of your clients.

Poor supervision and accountability. A lot of hypnotherapists are not members of any professional associations, they just practice day-to-day, do their own thing, and never associate with other hypnotists. They say that isolation breeds insanity. Perhaps in this case it breeds quakery.

Because the field of hypnosis is largely unregulated, its professionals often have poor supervision and accountability. I think it is important to contribute to the hypnosis associations, and to reap the benefits they offer. I am a member of a variety of different organizations, I attend their conferences and conventions, read their newsletters, submit my own articles, attend classes and even teach some. Because of this, my skills have been enhanced and I have made great friends whom I can call upon should I ever have a question or concern about one of my clients or a method or approach. I encourage you to become involved with other hypnotists, on one level or another.

Profit. I am a capitalist, and I am all in favor of profit. I like making money, because I get to pay my mortgage, feed my kids, visit my out-of-state friends and do fun things when I have money in my pocket. However, despite this ideal, we need to realize that over-emphasis on the profit motive can sometimes lead to quackery.

For example, let's say you believe that Anton Mesmer was right; the true reason why we have problems is that our magnetic energy forces are out of whack. Despite the fact that this concept has been scientifically disproved, let's say you have clients who are depressed, and you say, "Hey, buy this magnet from me and wear it; it will cure your depression." You have entered the field of quackery because what you are really doing is selling magnets for profit, not helping the person.

Another common 'for profit' practice is deliberately prolonging the time spent with a client in a session or through multiple sessions, so as to gain more fees. If you can cure something in one session, do so. People pay usually cash for hypnosis services, and to retain clients because they have the ability to pay us does not build autonomy, but leads to quackery. To provide services for any and every condition, even if there is no demonstrated efficacy, just because it is profitable, is quackery, not to mention unethical. The profit motive drives the engine of our society most of the time in a positive and in a good way, but sometimes the profit motive can lead to quackery.

Please understand that not all of these situations always lead to poor practice, but we need to be aware that they all have the potential to open up the doorway to quackery.

<u>CONCLUSION</u>

Back to the Beginning

I was going to write THE END at this point, but I decided that 'Back to the Beginning' was far more appropriate. Even though I think this book is quite comprehensive, it is still a basic, beginning course for those without prior experience in hypnosis. Yes, it has taught you about the mechanics of hypnosis as well as some of the nuances, but - at least hopefully - it is only the beginning of your hypnotic training journey.

I hope you take from these pages a set of skills that you can use, but also build upon, and that you don't end your education in hypnosis here. Go on to read more materials, watch videos and attend live trainings by other professionals. I took several different basic hypnotherapy courses when I first learned hypnosis, and this was quite beneficial because everyone has a little different perspective or approach, and being able to evaluate multiple viewpoints has allowed me to more fully form my own opinions, perspectives, styles and approaches. And I still attend classes, both basic and advanced. I am always looking to learn something new, and I like to see how other people teach people who are new to the profession of hypnotism. The world of hypnosis is truly exciting, and I am sure you will enjoy exploring it further.

It is also a world which many find confusing. Hypnotists sometimes contradict themselves and each other, and often cannot even agree on the definition of hypnosis itself. I encourage you to embrace this confusion, as it is one of the most important gateways to understanding, and to make your own informed judgments based on education and practice experience.

If right now you are beginning to feel empowered and exciting and can see yourself studying hypnosis with a passion and enjoying acquiring these new skills and understandings, then the goals Nathan and I had when we began this book are accomplished.

Wishing you the best of luck on your hypnotic journey,

Richard K. Nongard, LMFT/CCH
Nathan Thomas, C.Ht.

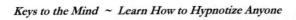

Made in the USA
Lexington, KY
06 October 2013